课程研究前沿 总主编 崔允漷

技术赋能的课堂分析 石雨晨　杨晓哲　编

Technology-empowered Classroom Analysis

华东师范大学出版社
·上海·

图书在版编目(CIP)数据

技术赋能的课堂分析/石雨晨,杨晓哲编. —上海：华东师范大学出版社,2024. —(课程研究前沿).
ISBN 978-7-5760-5571-9

Ⅰ. G424.21-53

中国国家版本馆CIP数据核字第20258YE388号

技术赋能的课堂分析

编　　者　石雨晨　杨晓哲
策划编辑　彭呈军
责任编辑　张艺捷
责任校对　王丽平
装帧设计　刘怡霖

出版发行　华东师范大学出版社
社　　址　上海市中山北路3663号　邮编200062
网　　址　www.ecnupress.com.cn
电　　话　021-60821666　行政传真 021-62572105
客服电话　021-62865537
门市(邮购)电话 021-62869887
地　　址　上海市中山北路3663号华东师范大学校内先锋路口
网　　店　http://hdsdcbs.tmall.com

印 刷 者　上海锦佳印刷有限公司
开　　本　787毫米×1092毫米　1/16
印　　张　7.25
字　　数　152千字
版　　次　2025年2月第1版
印　　次　2025年2月第1次
书　　号　ISBN 978-7-5760-5571-9
定　　价　58.00元

出 版 人　王　焰

(如发现本版图书有印订质量问题,请寄回本社客服中心调换或电话021-62865537联系)

序言

课堂是学生学习与教师教学的重要时空。今天的课堂怎么样,决定着明天的世界如何发展。小小的课堂,充满着数不尽的奥秘。蓦然回首,每个人的人生都离不开课堂这块重要的基石。理解课堂、设计课堂、改变课堂是教育学人的出发点和归宿。

2022年11月11—12日,在风和日丽、万里晴空的日子里,教育部人文社会科学重点研究基地华东师范大学课程与教学研究所主办了第20届上海国际课程论坛,以此为契机,共同探讨与构建以学为中心的课堂生态,助推未来课堂教与学范式的转型。

本次论坛主题是"技术赋能的国际课堂分析:打开黑箱与重构课堂"。来自联合国教科文组织、哈佛大学、斯坦福大学、哥伦比亚大学、加州大学伯克利分校、牛津大学、剑桥大学、华盛顿大学、香港大学、北京大学等国际组织和大学的专家与学者们,以主旨发言、圆桌论坛、专题报告为主要形式,着重探讨了五个议题,分别是:新技术时代下的课堂分析、多种取径的课堂研究和数据分析方法、化数据为证据的课堂分析、技术驱动的教师专业发展、课堂教学研究范式。诸多顶级专家学者在此思想汇聚。论坛通过线上线下结合,论坛吸引了5万余位与会者,形成了广泛的交流。

对深入课堂学习过程的理解方面,迪安娜·库恩(Deanna Kuhn)教授指出,通过观察和参与富有逻辑的对话,能够有效地丰富和深化人们的思维。同时指出,青少年通过一对一或小组间的辩论可以增强他们的责任感和对话能力,这对于未来的民主社会至关重要。克里斯汀·豪(Christine Howe)教授的文章探讨了在课堂上通过小组合作学习来促进学生学习的效果。她的研究表明,当学生在小组中持有不同的观点并通过高质量的对话交流时,小组合作能显著提升学习效果。

在科学教育方面,乔纳森·奥斯本(Jonathan Osborne)教授讨论了在信息泛滥和后真相时代,科学教育的重要性及其面临的挑战。他强调了培养学生评估信息和专家可信度的能力,认为科学教育应当教授基本的数字媒体素养和科学知识,以帮助学生在信息泛滥的环境中做出明智的判断。马西亚·林(Marcia Linn)教授指出知识整合过程包括引出学生的想法、发现新想法、区分和整理想法。这一过程通过在线环境中的模型、模拟和图表互动来实现,帮助学生深入理解科学现象。

基于多种视角的课堂分析方面,陈高伟教授的研究提出了一种基于可视化分析支持的教学视频观看方式,以促进教师对课堂对话片段的反思、理解和讨论。刘良华教授的研究聚焦于课堂回音的策略,包括重复或归纳、追问或征询、点评或补充。这些策略不仅可以为学生的学习提供及时反馈,还能提升教师的专业发展水平和教学质量。安桂清教授阐述了课堂形态分析与重构,关注课堂时空、课堂活动、课堂内容及其价值选择。徐瑾劼副教授等选取课件视角,打开对于课堂的另一种观察与理解。肖思汉副教授探索了中国课堂上的"回音"话语。石雨晨副教授的研究通过文献研究和专家论证,提出了课堂分析领域的十大前沿问题,围绕价值引领、实施操作、教学教研三个方面,旨在推动课堂分析领域的持续探索和创新。杨晓哲副教授基于高品质课堂智能分析系统,分析了大规模课堂视频数据,初步揭示了中国课堂教学现象和学习规律。

技术是时代发展的重要底色。如何打开课堂"黑箱",如何超越人类的听力、视力借用新技术的力量透视课堂,为实现高质量育人提供数据与证据,这应是教育学界同仁努力解决的重大课题。聚焦"技术"与"课堂分析",合力探讨超越传统听课、观课的"数课"成为了未来发展的重要趋势之一。

如上所述,本书汇聚了诸多学者们的研究发现与多元观点。本书能顺利出版,归功于各篇的作者们,我们及团队进行了论文汇集与进一步的整理,并于2024年出版。由于时间和水平有限,难免存在一些不足,恳请广大读者批评指正。让我们共同探索与期待,打开课堂黑箱,理解学习奥秘,重塑课堂新样态。

石雨晨　杨晓哲

2024 年 7 月

目录

时代变革下的课堂分析

Enhancing Teacher Guidance with an Authoring and Customizing Environment (ACE) to Promote Student Knowledge Integration (KI)
.... 美国加州大学伯克利分校　Marcia Linn　003

课堂形态分析及其重构：范式转换的视角
.... 华东师范大学　安桂清　014

Science Education in the Age of Misinformation
.... 美国斯坦福大学　Jonathan Osborne　026

课堂教与学的革新

转轴拨弦三两声：探索中国课堂上的"回音"话语
.... 华东师范大学　肖思汉　035

Interdisciplinarity for Enhanced Teaching and Learning of Science: Perspectives from School-Based Projects in the United Kingdom
.... 英国牛津大学　Sibel Erduran　050

技术驱动的教师发展

Group Work in Classrooms: Dialogue, Reflection and Positive Learning Outcomes
.... 英国剑桥大学　Christine Howe　061

可视化分析支持的教师专业发展：以课堂视频数据为例
.... 香港大学　陈高伟　068

课件分析视域下的教与学：打开课堂教学黑箱的另一种路径
.... 上海师范大学　徐勤劼　申昕　073

课堂回音与教师发展
.... 华东师范大学　刘良华　086

课堂分析的未来走向

国际课堂分析的十大前沿问题
.... 华东师范大学　石雨晨　093

基于人工智能技术的大规模课堂分析
.... 华东师范大学　杨晓哲　098

How Can We Equip Teenagers with Skills and Values of Reasoned and Respectful Discourse?
.... 美国哥伦比亚大学　Deanna Kuhn　106

时代变革下的课堂分析

Enhancing Teacher Guidance with an Authoring and Customizing Environment (ACE) to Promote Student Knowledge Integration (KI)

Professor Marcia C. Linn

University of California, Berkeley

Abstract

The talk addresses my work in the area of science education and Knowledge Integration, with a particular focus on enhancing teacher guidance with an Authoring and Customizing Environment to promote student Knowledge Integration. The work is conducted in an Authoring and Customizing Environment, an online environment that supports authoring by all members of the partnership. We also work closely with our teacher researchers to build teacher tools that enable them to teach effectively with the ACE or the Authoring and Customizing Environment. Effective instruction designed using the Authoring and Customizing Environment involves eliciting, discovering, distinguishing, and sorting out ideas.

Keywords: knowledge integration; science education; web-based inquiry science environment

The talk will address the work that I've been doing in the area of science education and Knowledge Integration. I really want to thank my colleagues in China who have contributed to this work. The talk will focus on enhancing teacher guidance with an Authoring and Customizing Environment to promote student Knowledge Integration. Our work is informed by the Knowledge Integration pedagogy. We use this pedagogy to guide the design of our instruction as well as to guide the design of professional development of our assessments and of the classroom interaction processes that support this work.

Our work is conducted in an Authoring and Customizing Environment. (Figure 1). This is an online environment, and it supports authoring by all members of the partnership (see https://wise.berkeley.edu/).

We have computer scientists who advanced the authoring environment and make it easier and easier for everyone in the partnership to contribute to the curriculum materials that we build for students. We also work closely with our teacher researchers to build teacher tools that

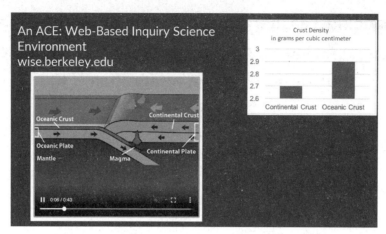

Figure 1. An ACE: Web-based inquiry science environment

enable them to teach effectively with the ACE or the Authoring and Customizing Environment.

Some of the teacher tools that can be used are listed here (Figure 2). Teachers can, in real time see how their students are doing. They can follow the progress of their students as they work through these materials. And as you'll see, as I talk about some of the units that students use, students work at their own pace usually in partnership with another student, and they write their responses in the authoring environment, and therefore teachers can see how they're doing.

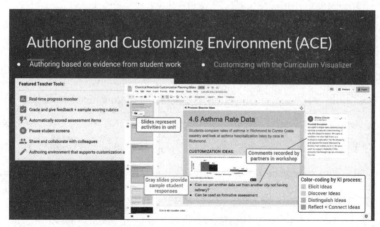

Figure 2. Teacher tools in ACE

In addition, the teacher tools include grading tools as well as automatically scored assessment items. There are tools that allow teachers to share and collaborate with colleagues. And finally, the authoring environment allows the teachers to customize the instruction. In Figure 2, you can see an example of the customizing environment. In this environment, each step in the instruction is color coded to indicate the process, the Knowledge Integration process, that is contributing to that step.

There are four Knowledge Integration processes that we design our instruction to support (Figure 3). We support students to really express all of their ideas in the eliciting idea step (Figure 4). And then we support students to discover new ideas. And I'll talk a little bit about the way that students can discover ideas using models and simulations and graphing and all sorts of hands-on activities as well. When they have all these great ideas, they need to really figure out which ones are most valuable.

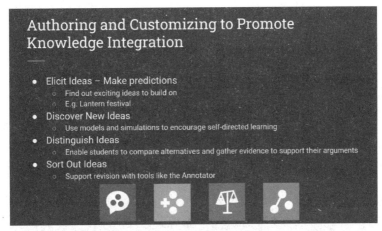

Figure 3. Four Knowledge Integration processes

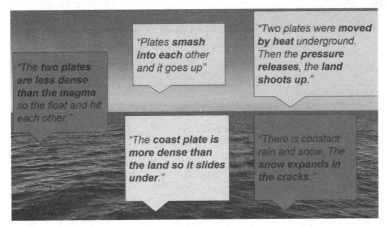

Figure 4. Student ideas

Our third process involves distinguishing among these ideas. And finally, we encourage students to reflect on this process and put everything together, because it really matters which ideas they want to maintain as they think about these important science concepts that they're studying. When teachers customize the instruction after looking at the student work, they can keep track of which Knowledge Integration process is being supported by the particular step. So here we have a step that involves discovering ideas. And here in the Curriculum Visualizer, they have some student work that the teacher is using to think about how to modify or improve the step. They also have comments from other teachers as to how this has worked. Therefore, they work together to customize the instruction after the lesson has been taught.

Now we will turn to ACE — the Web-based Inquiry Science Environment — which is an important Authoring and Customizing Environment that we use in our work. In ACE, students can interact with models and simulations. Here is a model of plate movement for our plate tectonics unit (Figure 5). They can work with graphs. For example, here is a bar graph that compares the density of different parts of the crusts in plate tectonics (Figure 6). And finally,

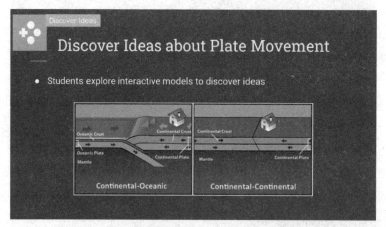

Figure 5. A model of plate movement for plate tectonics unit

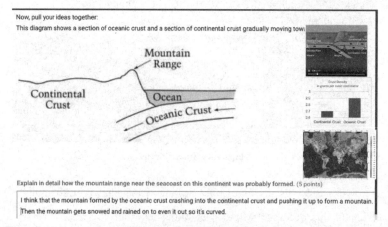

Figure 6. A bar graph comparing density of different parts of crusts in plate tectonics

they can interact with graphs and models and maps. This map is a particularly interesting one because it can show the pattern of volcanoes, earthquakes, and other changes in landforms so students can get a deeper understanding of plate tectonics. (Figure 1)

An important part of all of our work, of course, is eliciting student ideas. And let's look at a way we elicit student ideas in the plate tectonics unit. In this unit, students are asked to respond to this question (Figure 7). The question says this is Mount Hood. It is a part of the mountain range called the Cascades on the West Coast in Oregon. Explain how you think the mountain formed. Be as specific and detailed as you can.

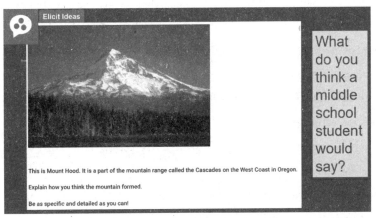

Figure 7. Question to elicit student ideas

I invite you to write down a few ideas you think a middle school student might have. Think of what a middle school student might say if asked to explain how this mountain was formed. Take a moment to think about what factors a middle school student might consider in explaining the formation of a mountain, or whether they might even say they don't think mountains were formed, they just exist.

Let's look at a few responses that our students give (Figure 4). One student says the two plates are less dense than the magma, so they float and hit each other. Another student says plates smash into each other and it goes up. Another student says there is constant rain and snow. The snow expands in the cracks. So that student is essentially saying that the snow is forming the mountain. Another idea that students often express is the coast plate is more dense than the land, so it slides under. This student is starting to think about density, as was the first student. And these are important factors for the teacher to take into consideration in planning class discussions and lessons. Another comments two plates were moved by heat underground. Then the pressure releases, the land shoots up. This student is starting to think about what is going deeper under the ground and not just about the plates that are moving on the surface.

All of these ideas are so rich and valuable for teachers as they think about how to help their students understand this complex topic. And from our Knowledge Integration perspective, we know that it's super important to pay attention to each and every idea that students have and to build on those ideas, because students have spent time carefully developing these thoughts and they have a connection to them that often they don't have if they just read something in a book. We therefore help students connect the ideas that they've developed on their own, thinking about these topics, to the ideas that might be more scientifically accurate but not familiar to the students because we want students to feel that the work that they've done about the topic is important. And it may differ from the kinds of things that have eventually come up in the research, but many of the ideas that students have were held at some point or another by scientists. This process of Knowledge Integration is a very important one for supporting students to get deeper understanding of scientific phenomenon.

In these units governed by this ACE students have, after they express their many ideas, got to discover new ideas, so they can use the models to see how plate movement occurs and to understand the processes that lead to one plate and another behaving in a certain way. And they can also express and study factors such as density and the movement of the magma. So here is an example of one of the answers that a student gave to this question (Figure 6).

The student has some very interesting ideas about how the mountain formed. And the way we react to that idea is that we use our Knowledge Integration scoring rubric to think about how the student is progressing in integrating their ideas (Figure 8). This rubric rewards students for

KI Categories	Score
Complex Link: Two or more scientifically complete and valid connections between normative ideas	5
Full Link: One scientifically complete and valid connection between two normative ideas	4
Partial Link: Unelaborated connections OR valid connections insufficient to explain	3
No Link: Scientifically non-normative or vague ideas or links	2
Irrelevant or Off Task	1

Knowledge Integration Scoring: Rewards links among ideas

Figure 8. Knowledge Integration scoring rubric

making more and more links among ideas and for using evidence to support the links that they made. We score these responses along this five-point scale with a three being a partial link, unelaborated connections or valid connections insufficient to explain, which is pretty much the answer that we have here. And then we give students guidance to help them integrate their ideas to the next level of the rubric.

For example, one kind of guidance that this student might get would be: "Jo, add details to your explanation. How does the density of the two plates affect their movement? Check out Step 3.5 for a hint. Then revise your explanation." This student might go back to Step 3.5 to learn more about density and then make a revision to their response. And we'll talk in a minute about what we do after we look at the revisions that students make.

Here's the kind of revision processes that we've observed so far in our research. Many students have quite a lot of difficulties thinking about how to revise their ideas. Think about your own experience. How do you feel when you have to revise a paper? Well, students often feel the same way. They don't feel like they really want to make many changes. And yet, revision is a really great way to learn how to make sense of a complex scientific phenomenon. As you get more information, then you can revise the explanation to be more sophisticated and to incorporate more evidence. What we find is that some students do exactly that, they integrate a new idea. Here's an example of a response which is in white and the revision which is in red (Figure 9).

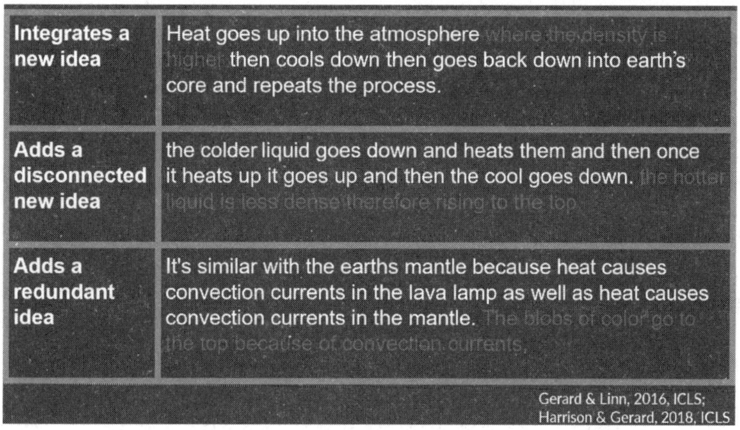

Integrates a new idea	Heat goes up into the atmosphere where the density is higher then cools down then goes back down into earth's core and repeats the process.
Adds a disconnected new idea	the colder liquid goes down and heats them and then once it heats up it goes up and then the cool goes down. the hotter liquid is less dense therefore rising to the top.
Adds a redundant idea	It's similar with the earths mantle because heat causes convection currents in the lava lamp as well as heat causes convection currents in the mantle. The blobs of color go to the top because of convection currents.

Gerard & Linn, 2016, ICLS;
Harrison & Gerard, 2018, ICLS

Figure 9. An example of a response in white and revision in red

A student writes in the white words 'heat goes up into the atmosphere, then cools down then goes back down into earth's core and repeats the process'. After getting hint or guidance, the student adds more ideas that integrate and explain the answer better, saying the 'heat goes up into the atmosphere where the density is higher than cools down then go back down into the earth's core where it is less dense and repeats the process'. So that's the kind of thing that we're looking for. Many students however, instead add a disconnected new idea which indicates that they were making a big effort to try to understand the situation and they haven't yet found enough evidence to really figure out how to connect the ideas or whether these are the right ideas to connect. So, for example, in this answer the student started by saying 'the colder liquid goes down and heats them and then once it heats up it goes up and then the cool goes down'. And after being asked to revise, the student adds 'the hotter liquid is less dense therefore rising to the top'. So really, two disconnected ideas.

Another phenomenon often happens when students are asked to revise is they just add a redundant idea. This student at the bottom of the slide says 'it's similar with the earth's mantle because heat causes convection currents in the lava lamp as well as heat causes convection currents in the mantle.' The blobs of color go to the top because of convection currents. The student essentially repeats ideas about confection currents in the revision process.

An interesting question is how can we help students make more productive revisions? These three kinds of revisions are common. In fact, integrating a new idea occurs only about 50% of the time. So, in thinking about how to improve students' revision processes, we have looked to the teachers. What do teachers do as they walk around the classroom and talk to students to guide them and to help them think about how to revise. Here's an example of a revision that a student makes as a result of talking with their teacher. So, the student basically adds a lot of very elaborated ideas as a result of the conversation. And as you can see here, the student says 'this happens because the oceanic plate is denser than the continental one. The subduction that is happening in the ocean near a continent then results in a volcano forming. Because Mount Hood is near the boundary between a continental and oceanic plate it caused this volcano mountain to emerge'.

This is an interesting and major revision, and it was developed as a result of a conversation with the teacher. And we wondered whether there was a way that we could support students to have these kinds of conversations, even if the teacher didn't have time to talk to each and every one of them. What we noted is that the teacher was really helping students think about what it means to revise, because it seemed like if we look at those examples before where students add a redundant or irrelevant idea that maybe they don't fully understand what it means to do revision, to really improve a response by adding evidence and sorting out the ideas.

We've thought hard about how to accomplish that, and we built what we call the

Annotator. (Figure 10). In the annotator, students are presented with a possible response written by one of their peers. It's actually a response that was written by a peer, although not necessarily one in the class that the student is in. And then, students are asked to think about how to guide the person who wrote this explanation in order to revise it effectively.

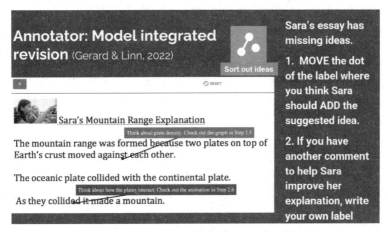

Figure 10. Annotator: Model integrated revision

The student is asked to move the dot of the label where they think Sara should add the suggested ideas. The student has two ideas here to add, and they can also create their own ideas, so they could add a third, fourth, or fifth idea. And then that's what they're told to do. If you have another comment to help Sara improve her explanation, write your own label. We had students use this annotator and then after that, do a revision of their own response.

Think for a moment. What do you think would happen if students had this experience and then were asked to write their own explanation? Do you think they would write a better explanation, make a better revision after working with the annotator? Or do you think it would be pretty much the same as the kind of guidance that you saw before where we guide students to find evidence relevant to the level of their Knowledge Integration?

Think for a moment, make a prediction. Do you think the annotator would be more helpful, or do you think it would be better to give the kind of guidance that we showed you before where students are suggested to go to a new step or to a new model to think about a different idea? Well, what we found is very interesting. For students who already were at a level three to four, essentially already had some links in their explanation, the annotator was a little bit effective, but not as effective as for students who had very few links who were at the zero, one or two level. For those students, the annotator was very effective. And I think that really supports our hypothesis that those students need a model of revision. Once they had a model to revise their explanation, they were more likely to make a really good revision and to add ideas that ultimately move them up the Knowledge Integration rubric to a higher score.

I also talked about how the next step in the Knowledge Integration process is to help students discover new ideas. And often, this is a challenging process. You saw some responses to questions where students mentioned lava lamps. One of the ways that we help students discover new ideas is actually to have them watch a lava lamp where blobs of oil rise and fall depending on their density. That image, as you can see in those examples, is actually helpful for students to think about density and connect it back to plate movement and to why one plate might go under another plate.

Finally, it's very important for students to distinguish all these ideas because obviously, if we give students a whole bunch of ideas and don't help them really figure out which ones are supported by the evidence that they're gathering, they might revert back to the ideas that we elicited at the beginning. Because after all, they've held on to those ideas for a long time and this unit might've only been going on for a week or two. In order for students to really consolidate their knowledge to connect their new ideas to the ones that they already have, activities that allow them to distinguish ideas are very important. And as you saw in our revision example, revising ideas is an important part of that process of distinguishing ideas.

It is also complicated when students get new evidence and are encouraged to use that to distinguish ideas, they sometimes revise their explanations and sometimes they decide to tackle an idea on or to say the same thing in a new way. Therefore, distinguishing ideas is a very important process and the distinguishing ideas activity gives students support for maybe a new idea. However, just supporting the new idea without consolidating all of that information that has come before, we found is frequently not sufficient.

A final activity in this Knowledge Integration process involves sorting out ideas. And the annotator has proven to be a good tool for helping students to sort out their ideas because it illustrates how you look at the ideas that you have and consider ways to decide which ones are more valuable or which ones have more evidence to support them.

Effective instruction designed using the Authoring and Customizing Environment involves eliciting, discovering, distinguishing, and sorting out ideas. There are many books and papers available about Knowledge Integration to learn more about how this process works. We also have papers about how we design the assessments and how the proper professional development process can support teachers to be effective users of Knowledge Integration (see Related

Publications below).

Related Publications

Gerard, L., Linn, M.C. (2022). Computer-based guidance to support students' revision of their science explanations. *Computers & Education*, 176, 104351.

Bradford, A., Bichler, S., & Linn, M. C. (2021). Designing a Workshop to Support Teacher Customization of Curricula. In E. de Vries, J. Ahn, & Y. Hod (Eds.), *Proceedings of the 15th International Conference of the Learning Sciences 2021* (pp. 100–115). Nashville, Tennessee: ISLS.

Gerard, L., Wiley, K., Bradford, A., Chen, J.K., Lim-Breitbart, J., & Linn, M. (2020). Impact of a Teacher Action Planner that Captures Student Ideas on Teacher Customization Decisions. In Gresalfi, M. and Horn, I. S. (Eds.), *Proceedings of the 14th International Conference of the Learning Sciences 2020*, Volume 4 (pp. 2077–2084). Nashville, Tennessee: ISLS.

Nie, Y., Xiao, Y., Fritchman, J. C., Liu, Q., Han, J., Xiong, J., & Bao, L. (2019). Teaching towards knowledge integration in learning force and motion. *International Journal of Science Education*, 41(16), 2271–2295.

Pei, X., Jin, Y., Zheng, T., & Zhao, J. (2020). Longitudinal effect of a technology-enhanced learning environment on sixth-grade students' science learning: The role of reflection. *International Journal of Science Education* 42(2), 271–289.

Wiese, E.S., & Linn, M.C. (2021). "It Must Include Rules" Middle School Students' Computational Thinking with Computer Models in Science. ACM Transactions on Computer-Human Interaction (TOCHI), 28(2), 1–41.

Li, W., Linn, M. (2022). Responses of rural Chinese teachers to workshops on culturally relevant constructivist pedagogy. *Proceedings of the 16th International Conference of the Learning Sciences 2022* (pp. 1253–1256). Nashville, Tennessee: ISLS.

Wiley, K. J., Dimitriadis, Y., Bradford, A., & Linn, M. C. (2020). From theory to action: Developing and evaluating learning analytics for learning design. *Proceedings of the 10th International Conference on Learning Analytics & Knowledge (LAK '20)* (pp. 569–578). ACM. https://doi.org/doi.org/10.1145/3375462.3375540.

课堂形态分析及其重构：范式转换的视角

安桂清

【摘要】随着课堂研究范式的转换，在由"间接测量"到"直接研究"的发展历程中，课堂这一"黑箱"逐渐被打开。传统的基于师生报告的问卷调查逐渐被包括视频记录在内的课堂观察所代替。然而，直接查看教室仍然是烦琐、昂贵和侵入性的，以人工智能技术支撑的课堂分析为便捷化、规模化、非介入式的课堂整体形态研究提供了支撑。课堂研究有待超越传统研究范式对教师特质或教学实践的考察，在开辟技术支持的新的方法论基础上，对包括内容形态、活动形态和时空形态在内的课堂形态做出整体刻画与分析，并最终借助分析结果探索课堂形态重构的路径。

【关键词】教学研究范式；课堂视频研究；课堂形态；课堂智能分析

【作者简介】安桂清/华东师范大学课程与教学研究所教授、书记

Analysis and Reconstruction of Classroom State: Perspective from Paradigm Shift

AN Guiqing

(Institute of Curriculum and Instruction, East China Normal University, Shanghai 200062)

Abstract: With the transformation of classroom research paradigm, classroom research has experienced the development process from "indirect measurement" to "direct research". In this process, the "black box" of classroom is gradually opened. The traditional questionnaire where teacher and student report on teaching practice has gradually been replaced by classroom observation, including video recordings. However, looking directly into classrooms remains generally complex, costly and intrusive. The classroom analysis supported by AI technology provides support for the convenient, large-scale, non-interventional research on the overall state of the classroom. Classroom research needs to go beyond investigation on the characteristics of teachers or teaching practice, and on the basis of developing a new methodology supported by technology, make a comprehensive description and analysis of the classroom state, including content state, activity state and space-time state. Finally, with the analysis results, researchers expect to find the path of classroom state reconstruction.

Keywords: teaching research paradigm; classroom video research; classroom state; intelligence classroom analysis

教学的复杂性和基于情境的性质给研究者们理解课堂带来了极大的挑战性。因为作为一个复杂系统,"其所包含的信息并不是存在于构成这个系统的各自为营的组成部分,而是遍布于它们联结性网络的模式之中"。[1]换言之,课堂教学的多种实践活动是在与各种要素交织的网络中同时发生的。然而回顾教学研究的历史,很长一段时期该领域是围绕教师的特质或教学的互动实践展开的。倘若以单独分解和相互隔离的要素为研究对象,去捕捉和描述课堂的现实表现,虽能深化对教与学的理解,但依然无法反映课堂的整体面貌及其特征。正如菲利普·W·杰克逊(Jackson, P. W.)在其课堂研究的经典之作《课堂生活》中所表达的那样:"除了观察教学互动的主要特征以及课程的总体设计,我们也万万不能忽略那些转瞬即逝的事情的意义,也就是学生打个哈欠或者教师皱下眉头那样的事。与人们最初的印象不同,这一类事件恰恰包含了有关课堂生活的丰富信息。"[2]佐藤学从另一侧面揭示了这种复杂性:"像教学这么复杂的、日常性、长期性的沟通过程之中,眼睛看不见的因素和感化比看得见的行为拥有更重要的作用。"[3]所以要打开课堂的黑箱,需要具有开创性的新的方法来驾驭其固有的复杂性,确保教学活动研究的数据标识能与其所处的境脉相联系。为此,超越传统的教学研究,以课堂研究作为专门的研究领域,通过探索教学活动、数据标识与课堂境脉等之间的共存关系,从而对课堂的形态做出整体勾画,并分析其特征和赋予其意义,这将是课堂研究的发展趋势。

一、迈向课堂形态分析:教学研究范式[①]转换的结果

"课堂"作为专门研究领域的兴起很大程度上受到教学研究范式转换的影响。正是在教学研究范式的转换中,研究者被拉回到教学的现实世界,更确切地说是回到每一个真实的课堂。

(一)范式转换与课堂黑箱的打开

自20世纪60年代盖奇(Gage, N. L.)在第一版的《教学研究手册》中开始探讨教学研究范式以来,不同文化情境中的学者对转换中的研究范式虽有不同的表述,但在逐渐接近并直面真实而复杂的课堂挑战这一点上却显示出惊人的一致性。

以美国学者多伊尔(Doyle, W.)和日本学者佐藤学教授的经典划分为例,多伊尔将教学研究范式分为过程—产出范式,中介—过程范式和生态—文化范式。[4]过程—产出范式的基本旨趣在于在严格的科学的统计方法基础上寻求教师教学行为与特征和学生成就之间的关系。该范式把教学作为技术性的过程加以控制,通常被认为遮蔽了教学的复杂性,剥夺了教与学的创造性,助长了教学的划一化。中介—过程范式的基本旨趣在于透视教师认知或学生学习

机制在教师教学行为和学生学习结果之间的调节作用。然而对教师认知的研究忽略了主流的教学文化以及时间(任教时间)和空间(教室、学校、社区以及国家)对教师教学行为的塑造。生态—文化范式的基本旨趣在于像杰克逊在《课堂生活》中展现的那样,采用自然主义的方法对课堂事件和过程进行描述,并在与环境脉络互动中理解与诠释课堂的意义。生态—文化范式承认教学是一个满载了文化、社会意义的活动,研究者需要从跨学科的角度开展复杂的课堂研究。佐藤学用黑匣子、玻璃盒和潘多拉盒三种隐喻概括教学研究的范式。[5]"黑匣子"范式以定量的方法探讨教学过程诸要素之功能的因果关系。"玻璃盒"范式则如透过玻璃窗观察课堂,试图基于对课堂观察的质性研究取得教学过程的理论解读。无论是"黑匣子"还是"玻璃盒",研究者并未走进课堂去钻研师生直面的实践课题。而"潘多拉盒"范式则是指研究者亲临课堂,直面课堂事实的复杂性与丰富性,直面教师实践的难度与可能性,在复杂的混沌中满怀"希望"地求得实践性问题的解决。两位学者对教学研究范式的论述可谓异曲同工。这种趋势在第三、第四版的《教学研究手册》中得到强化。艾森哈特(Eisenhart,M.)在第四版《教学研究手册》中进一步发展了在第三版《教学研究手册》中提出的民族志方法。针对当代社会日益深刻的全球化与快速的人口流动所导致的个体文化处境的流变性与复杂性,艾森哈特指出多地点或多对象的民族志研究更能解释课堂中的行动对参与者的意义以及同更大范围内的社会行动和结构的联系。[6]国内学者从我国教学论转型的角度也强调了打开课堂"黑箱"、直面课堂本身的迫切性。如王鉴教授提出应建立"课堂教学论",使教学研究从"文本"走向"实事"。[7]钟启泉教授认为课堂是交织着多重声音的世界,是一个社会的、政治的、历史的、文化的空间。[8]他先后出版了"课堂研究三部曲"——《读懂课堂》《课堂研究》《课堂转型》,试图为"课堂"这一专门研究领域的确立提供理论视角。

综上所述,教学研究范式的转换是逐渐打开课堂黑箱、际遇课堂真实的历程。在研究信念上,课堂的情境性、高复杂性和交互性特征逐渐得到确认。与此同时,研究者与教师在共同直面课堂的复杂性、矛盾和挑战时,过往研究所助长的专业研究人员和教师的对立逐渐消解,研究者在方法论层面得以超越对"教学"的间接测量,开启对"课堂"的直接研究。

(二) 从间接测量到直接研究

除课堂观的转变外,教学研究范式的转换还体现为方法论上的转变。由于传统上对课堂的解释通常依赖于间接测量手段,例如教师和学生报告不同课堂教学实践的存在或频率的问卷调查。[9]这类调查所反映的主要是课堂主体对于课堂的感知、理解、体验,而不是课堂本身,因此往往难以全面、真正地揭示课堂的实际面貌。有时在通过教师的自我报告衡量教学时甚至面临与真实情况不符的挑战,因为这些报告可能更多是教师的社会合意反应。[10]同时,作为一项复杂的活动,教学从来都不是一个线性的过程,许多教学实践通常同时发生,每一个都很难单独分解和隔离,而间接测量定义在纸上的衡量标准究竟在多大程度上反映了真实的教学实践,争议在所难免。因此迫切需要通过直接记录对教学过程进行细致而准确的描述与分析。

几十年来,研究者持续探索利用课堂观察这一衡量工具关注特定的教师行为和相互作用的定性分析,特别是通过视频观察捕捉更全面的课堂信息,发挥其在多次观看或慢动作分析等方面的灵活性,开展更为全面、细致和富有针对性的研究。以下述国际课堂视频研究项目为例(见表1),我们可以看到课堂研究方法的进展与特征。

表1 国际课堂视频研究项目的主要特点(部分)[11]

研究项目	涉及国家	前/后设计	录像课数量	每个国家的教师数	共同评估标准	共同的主题	课件	学生问卷	教师问卷	教师日志
GTI	8	×	2	85	×	×	×	×	×	×
TIMSS 1995	3		1	70—100	×				×	
TIMSS 1999	7		1	70—100	×				×	
LPS	14		10	3			×			

使用视频技术对不同国家的教学进行调查和比较始于1995年的TIMSS测验,当时只有日本、德国和美国三个国家参加,分析对象为三个国家的231节课堂视频。1999年的TIMSS视频研究扩展到7个国家,视频总量达到1000节课以上。为保证在跨文化环境中对教学实践有共同的理解,TIMSS还制定了课堂教学的共同评估标准。TIMSS视频研究激发了国家和国际层面对课堂视频研究的应用。学习者视角研究(Learner's Perspective Study,简称LPS)由澳大利亚墨尔本大学国际课堂研究中心的克拉克(David Clarke)教授发起,14个国家或地区参与,更多关注对课堂重要事件,如课堂指导、课堂练习、课堂总结等的研究,除视频记录和课件外,还通过对师生的广泛访谈收集了参与者对这些课堂事件的解释数据。[12]虽然LPS比TIMSS视频研究更加深入,然而同TIMSS相似,该项目也只探查了非常小的数学课堂样本。事实上,大多数利用视频技术的课堂研究都有着规模过小的局限性。2020年国际经合组织(OECD)发布了"全球教学洞察"(Global Teaching Insights,简称GTI)课堂视频分析项目的研究报告,该项目试图更加详细而深入地探查8个国家和地区的课堂教学特征。这种努力体现为:第一,相对于TIMSS视频研究中教师自由地选择教学内容拍摄视频,GTI收集的视频资料聚焦于同样的内容主题(一元二次方程),这使得课堂之间、国家之间更具可比性;第二,通过纵向设计监测一段时间教学前后学生在认知与非认知上的变化,将教学实践与学生学习结果联系起来;第三,运用多种教学测量手段,例如课件、教师与学生问卷、教师教学日志与课堂视频的收集和评分,以勾画更全面、更详细的教学图景。即便如此,GTI项目在反思自身的研究时,依然强调该研究的重点是通过新的研究方法,捕捉世界各地教学的丰富性、复杂性和多样性,以更好地理解教与学,而不是对"教学形态"(state of Teaching)的综合研究。[13]

(三）课堂智能分析对课堂形态的揭示

上述国际课堂视频分析研究项目通过对课堂实践的直接测量为研究人员进入课堂打开了一扇门。然而，直接查看课堂仍然是烦琐的、昂贵的和带有侵入性的。以常见的拍摄方式为例，每堂课可能要有三个机位去关注焦点的学生、全景的学生以及教师，拍摄教室的成本是高昂的，而且在后勤保障方面具有挑战性。同时，当如此多的机器、拍摄者进入课堂，整个教室的氛围、师生的教学状态必然会受到影响，视频研究的侵入性是显而易见的。不仅如此，对学生课堂数据的保护还需要研究者对研究伦理保持敏感。除此之外，对真实的课堂而言，视频所捕捉到的更多的是师生的教学实践，具体的课堂内容以及完整的课堂时空尚无法全部纳入。[14]如何使课堂研究更具便捷化、规模化和非介入性，这期待课堂研究方法的跃迁。

近年来，随着人工智能技术的发展，课堂智能分析对突破目前视频研究的瓶颈做了有益的尝试与探索。基于人工智能在图像识别、语音识别、行为识别和模式识别等技术功能模块的进展，课堂智能分析能够提供包含言语数据、行为数据、心理数据、生理数据、脑数据、学业数据等在内的多模态、全方位、长时段的课堂数据，[15]并借助一系列课堂全息算法，经由机器学习生成智能分析结果。课堂智能分析为整体把握课堂的形态奠定了方法论基础。"形态"指的是"事物的状态或表现形式"。同一人或事物往往以不同的状态存在。假如我们在比较长的时间段内加以连续考察，就可能发现某人或某事物的整体活动状态的特征。而所处的状态不同，反映了此人或此事物所持有或所彰显的价值或理念的差异。同理，所谓"课堂形态"即课堂的状态或表现形式。任何课堂总是处于某种状态或具备某种表现形式，因此，课堂形态是课堂的实际面貌和具体样子。课堂若连续处于某种状态，则该课堂便形成了一种相对稳定的形态，其背后往往反映了对"课堂应当怎样"的价值追求和理念选择。由此可见，对课堂形态展开研究是了解课堂实际面貌和具体样子，揭示其背后或显或隐的价值与理念的重要途径。以"课堂形态"这一反映课堂实然全貌的概念建构为契机，必将开创课堂研究的新局面。

二、课堂形态模型的构建

课堂形态通常被认为是对课堂结构的一种抽象描述。有研究者对课堂结构的要素做了归纳，并梳理出其不同的层次，认为其是由顶层的价值和理念、中层的内容和教法以及底层的时空和技术等要素构成。[16]课堂形态实际上是课堂结构的各个要素动态运行所呈现出的状态，由于其在运行中受到某种教育价值和理念的引领，课堂形态会相应地体现某些特征和价值取向。因而，课堂形态是在一定的教育价值和理念指导下，构成课堂的各个层面的结构化要素，包括在内容组织、教学活动、时空环境等之间形成的比较稳定的、模式化的关系及其在运行中所表现出的形式与状态。根据此界定，如左图所示，本研究尝试建构课堂形态的三维模型。

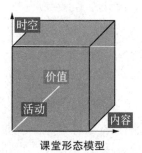

课堂形态模型

基于不同的价值选择,课堂形态会展现出不同的演进方向。比如,有学者从超越工业化社会的标准化课堂形态出发,期望建构大数据支持的大规模个性化教学形态,[17]为此翻转课堂、混合学习等"虚实融合"的教学活动、以"资源—学习者"配套为特征的个性化内容配置以及技术支持的学习空间建构就成为课堂形态演进的具体内涵。坚持素养导向、变革育人方式是我国新一轮课程改革的方向。课堂形态的变革也应以素养取向的课堂为价值追求,探索与素养培育相适应的课堂内容形态、活动形态和时空形态的重构。

课堂的活动形态是传统教学研究关注的重心,教与学的互动是其研究的焦点。但不同于把教与学视为被划分后相互排斥的对立面,从形态的视角看教与学是相互交织的,不可能存在单独的教。教是旨在促进学的一种特别的交流形式,"即使学习是由学生本人来实施的,教必须进行调整以支持学生的学习,而这在复杂的现代生活中主要意味着教的最关键任务是支持学生通过交流来处理复杂性"。[18]基于此,超越传统的教与学的割裂,课堂形态模型需要从教与学一体化的角度描述活动形态。借鉴学习科学对"教学"作为"学习环境的创设"这一新隐喻,[19]教师的"教"即是为学生的学习活动提供学习支持。因而超越传统的课堂实践,本研究拟从"学习活动—学习支持"两个对应的维度描述课堂的活动形态。

课堂的内容形态嵌入活动形态,是学生需要全身心关注的材料。课堂内容的来源与学校知识的选择有关。为超越传统的学科本位的教学内容,学生经验和社会生活一度在课堂中获得强调,然而近来对此又有不同的声音。比如,迈克·扬(Michael Young)等所宣称的学校应为所有学生提供的"强有力的知识"区别于学生带到学校的源于自身经验的知识,而是应回归以学术团体所积累的系统化的概念体系为特征的科目知识。[20]课堂中所呈现的究竟是何种类型的知识,这些知识虽与学科本身的发展紧密相关,但也因育人目标的价值取向不同而有所取舍。所以知识类型结构是课堂内容形态首要的分析维度。而不同类型的知识究竟以何种方式呈现给学生是课堂内容随之要展现的维度,这涉及内容的组织方式,知识的单位是怎样的?是以一个个零散的知识点串联,还是既能反映各种条理清晰的关系的核心,又能使事实更容易理解和有用的"概念锚点"。[21]内容载体的形式表现是什么,是习题训练、活动主题还是学习任务?透过这些形式反映出课堂内容的具体形态及其特征。

课堂时空形态传统上是不被重视的,因为人们并不认为时空是重要的变革力量。事实上,正像有的学者所指出的"也可能并不是因为教师不会教,而是因为整个教学环境设计不合理。我们早就应该把教育系统的失败归咎于教学环境,而不是教师"。[22]面对被老式的课桌椅、传统的装饰和固定的课时时间表充斥的教室,课堂时空形态的改变及其对教与学方式的影响日益受到广泛的关注。课堂时空形态的变革可以从时间形态和空间形态两个维度展开。

三、课堂形态的分析维度

由上述课堂形态模型出发,如表2所示,素养时代课堂形态的重构至少涉及如下维度:

表 2　素养时代课堂形态重构的维度

形态	维度	类　　型
内容形态	知识类型结构	内容性知识/方法性知识/价值性知识
	学习内容单位	知识点/大概念
	学习内容载体	练习/学习活动/学习任务
活动形态	学习活动	记中学、做中学、用中学、创中学
	学习支持	讲授/认知激发/社会情感支持
时空时态	时间形态	钟表时间/社会建构时间/虚拟时间
	空间形态	物理学习空间/虚拟学习空间/虚拟现实空间

（一）课堂内容形态的分析维度

课堂的内容形态源于不同形态的知识，反映出独特的内容单位，通过一定的内容载体加以呈现。因此，对课堂内容形态的描述主要包含知识类型结构、学习内容单位和学习内容载体三个方面。

1. 知识类型结构

从课堂形态的模型出发，为凸显素养培育的课堂转向，并体现内容形态、活动形态与时空形态之间的联系性与整体性，本研究所述的知识类型结构旨在超越传统的记忆性的事实性知识，强调学生获得理解并能在新情境中运用所学的方法性知识以及关乎学科价值和学习意义的价值性知识。[23] 知识类型结构的改变往往是各国课堂变革的前奏。以数学学科为例，OECD在分析 19 个国家和地区的国家课程标准和数学教科书后指出，相对于 TIMSS 1995 的数学框架，定量推理、高阶现实情境应用以及 21 世纪技能等成为素养时代许多国家的教学内容选择。[24] 三种类型的知识与学生对学科知识观念的理解、真实生活中的问题解决以及个体行为动力的精神支柱等素养的核心要义具有一定的对应关系，因此三类知识在课堂中的整体渗透是素养培育的前提。

2. 学习内容单位

知识点是传统课堂中学习内容的基本单位。面对浩渺的知识点，教师要想办法将其分配到有限的课时中，学生的学习则是吸收大量孤立的知识点，这不仅造成学生的学习负担，而且因其零散性也无法真正应用于需要的场合。大概念在学科中具有不同的类型和层级结构，从最底端的事实知识提取为主题，而后进一步抽象为概念，再演变发展至概念性理解。[25] 大概念以简驭繁，能够形成学生对学科知识最本质和最持久的理解，从而实现在不同情境中的相互迁移，包括学科内的迁移以及跨学科的互通。不同于像新手那样只认识孤立的路线，大概念以知识网络的形式架构和扩展学习内容，有助于使学生像专家一样思考，[26] 在遇到问题时，及时调取位于整体知识结构中的相应概念以解决问题。

3. 学习内容载体

直接讲授与机械练习是传统课堂的典型形态，"练习"因而成为传统课堂的内容载体。新世纪以来，基础教育课程改革力图通过学习活动设计改变学生被动接受的局面，然而学习活动作为内容载体，极易陷入"活动主义"，课堂表面热闹，却无法实现对活动背后所承载的知识内容的深度理解，在某些情况下，活动的割裂化、拼盘化、细碎化还进一步加剧了学生获得知识的散乱和无序。任务被认为是有效组织活动并使之实现进阶逻辑的重要线索。任务并未抛弃原来的活动，而是作为内容载体，以符合学科逻辑和学生身心发展规律的方式有效协调、组织和统领各项活动。因而，任务嵌套了学习内容，内蕴着学科大概念，有效执行任务或实现某个复杂产品是个体展现知识和专业能力的方式。威金斯和麦克泰格建议，在每一个单元教学中，至少应有一个核心的表现性任务按照 GRASPS（目标和角色、对象、情境、产品、标准）模式进行建构。[27]学生完成任务的过程既是学习活动的实施过程，亦是学生有组织、有进阶地获得学习内容的过程。

（二）课堂活动形态的分析维度

课堂活动形态揭示出课堂的实践结构。过去二十年，虽然基础教育课程改革通过倡导建立对话的课堂试图超越课堂实践的授—受传统，促进师生课堂互动，但同时，学生作为学习活动的主体地位经常被遗忘和消解。从"满堂灌"的课堂到"满堂问"的课堂展现的即是这一状况。当前，超越传统的课堂实践，由"学习活动—学习支持"两个对应的维度所描述的课堂活动形态亟待改变。

1. 学习活动

传统课堂主要以学生听讲、记忆、模仿、练习为主，"记中学"是其典型表现。过多的机械性记忆、重复性训练和被动式学习造成了学生沉重的学业负担。为此，新世纪以来，基础教育课程改革强调转变学生的学习方式，倡导开展"自主、合作、探究"的学习。但在实践中，由于忽视学习方式的丰富性，以及由于缺乏"自主、合作、探究"的学习方式与具体学科合二为一的策略和方法而导致的去学科化现象，[28]使得探究活动的浮泛、固化、虚假等问题亟待纠正。素养导向的学习在吸收以往学习活动组织与实施的经验基础上，通过强化学科实践，试图充分发挥实践的独特育人功能，加强知行合一、学思结合，倡导"做中学""用中学""创中学"，从而实现学习方式与学科特质深度耦合的学习活动。"做中学""用中学""创中学"这类学习活动具有情境性、具身性和整合性，与学科专家所从事的真实的专业实践类似，它体现了学生在其生命历程中对重叠、互补甚至冲突的文化实践中的多样行为库（repertories）的获得，[29]反映了素养时代学习的本质。

2. 学习支持

在"记中学"的课堂中主要体现为教师主导的"讲授"，严格说来其并不是与学生自主学习活动相对应的教师支持行为。新世纪以来的基础教育课程改革在强调学生的"自主、合作、探究"学习活动中,的确存在教师对学生对话、体验、讨论、合作、探究等学习过程的支持,但总体上是围绕师生互动展开的,并且主要强化的是教师对学生认知的激发与引导。素养取向的课堂期望教师的教学实践能够为学生创设支持性的学习环境,包括设计能够引导和导向学生学习的全部问题和任务性质的境脉支持,提供用于表征、组织、操作或者构建理解的学习工具与技术,提供从与学习主题相关的静态信息资源到社会化建构的动态发展资源,以及提供促进学生意义建构、过程管理、表达和反思的脚手架。[30]这些境脉、工具、资源与支架方面的支持指向的是学生理解力、分析力、创造力等高阶认知的发展。不仅如此,由于学生的发展不仅仅局限于理性认知,还包括情感、动机、意志等非认知因素的发展,因而教师的支持行为也应该包括对学生非认知的支持。以 OECD 的 GTI 视频研究为例,该项目提出了教师课堂教学实践中的社会情感支持(Socio-emotional support)概念。社会情感支持指向的是一种积极向上的氛围,学生在课堂上愿意冒险,并在智力或情感上接受挑战的支持性学习环境,从教师的角度表现为教师对学生的尊重,以及教师给予学生的鼓励与温暖。研究结果也表明,教师和学生表现出鼓励、温暖的教室和学校是学生有更高的学业成就和学习动机的地方。[31]社会情感支持与既往的认知激发性支持一样,都应该反映在教师的支持性教学实践中。

(三) 课堂时空形态的分析维度

相对于内容形态和活动形态的变革,课堂时空形态的改变更为缓慢,但其对课堂活动形态和内容形态的影响是不容小觑的。课堂时空形态的变革主要包括时间形态和空间形态两个方面。

1. 课堂时间形态

课堂时间形态的考察涉及对课堂钟表时间、社会建构时间和虚拟时间不同视角的分析。在以传统的钟表时间作为衡量尺度时,课堂时间被分割为可测量的线性的单位,随之教学内容也被精确分割进时间单位,以确保环环相扣,从而填满课堂的每一分钟和每一空间。因为个人的意愿无法脱离一定的时间规范,钟表时间无疑强化了学生的一致化行动,并由此加剧了学生与学生之间的竞争,个体自身的时间体验与意义建构被忽视。然而时间嵌入师生交往和成长的场域,是人的发展的结构性要素,课堂中儿童不同的时间观念和体验昭示着个体发展的多种可能性和不断生成性,因而,课堂时间具有社会建构性。社会建构时间强调尊重儿童内在的时间节律和时间体验,尊重个体学习的实际进程,在教学活动的制度安排上强调"宽松",微观上强调较强的弹性和适应性。随着信息技术革命、全球化和网络社会的发展,一种新的时间体验——虚拟时间被塑造。技术与时间之间的关系是一种"相互塑造",当人们以特定的方式使用技术时,会给技术赋予意义,从而塑造自己的时间体验。同时新技术能够重新配置人们体验时间的方式,以及在这一过程中人们运用信息技术媒介的方式。[32]虚拟时间是社会建构时间的延续,其体验更多变、更复杂、更快节奏。网络技术的使用促进了虚拟时空在课堂中的融入,时间边界的模糊性、时间使用的灵活性以及时间中的多任务处理成为虚拟时间的存在特征。[33]反映在课堂上,跨越时空边界,从线上学习到线上线下混合学习模式,虚拟时间不仅模糊并扩展了学生的学习时空与机会,同时潜在地增加了多种学习方式。网络所营造的虚拟时间还减少了人们对钟表时间的依赖,获得了更大的时间灵活性,学生能够以自己的步调展开学习或展示能力,教师具有确定何时何地履行专业责任的自主权,时间本质上是可变的,学习却是不变的。同时,高度数字化的环境使得不断中断当前任务和同时进行多项任务成为可能。学生通过搜索引擎、社交网络和即时活动消息可以同时开展多项活动。不过当学生坐在电脑前开始学习,他们是如何使用时间以及他们沉迷于何物可能不再像以前那样直接和明确。

2. 课堂空间形态

课堂空间形态的考察涉及对物理学习空间、虚拟学习空间和虚拟现实空间的分析。学校要建构与素养培育相适应的学习环境亟须对物理空间进行改造。提高空间总体的灵活性,并能够不断地基于学习需求对空间进行重新配置是其基本要求。美国西北大学学习科学研究所的创始人罗杰·尚克指出:"教室不复存在"是学校设计的语言。应当建立与学生的学习模式——计算机工作、与他人交谈、做事情相匹配的三种不同的学习环境:集中式工作环境、协作式工作环境和项目式工作环境。[34]将教学法融入空间,建立与学生学习需求相匹配的学习空间已成为学校设施改造的方向。比如建立学生大本营、合作孵化器、存储空间、专业和重点实验室、项目空间、户外学习空间、展示空间、突破空间、个人学习空间、小组学习空间、教师会议空间,[35]等等,这些积极的探索正在不断地颠覆传统的教室概念,扩展学习领域和合作区。虚拟学习空间主要是与实体性的物理学习空间相对的网络学习空间。通过网站平台的建设、资源的汇聚与推送、网络学习的指导与跟进、学习状态的分析与评价,虚拟学习空间能够有效助力学生的个性化学习和深度学习,并支持线上线下的融合学习,实现学校新型学习空间的重构。虚拟现实空间是技术与现实空间叠加而成的一种全新的模拟环境,学习者在完整地投入模拟环境时,能够获得沉浸性、交互性和构想性的体验。虚拟现实技术改变了知识的呈现方式和学习交互方式,增强了知识的可视性和学习过程的灵活性。学习空间的扩展有助于突破实体空间的容量和局限,通过虚拟构造特定的学习场景供学习者使用,实现基于学习需求的学习场景的转换。比如,戴维·索恩伯格(David Thornburg)在《学习场景的革命》中专门阐释了技术如何重塑其所建构的融合"营火"(听知识权威者讲述)、"水源"(在社交中相互学习)、"洞穴"(学会独立反思和思考)和"生活"(将学习带到实践中去)等各类学习场景并能自由切换的"教学全息甲板"这一学习环境,[36]以使学生在其中获得丰富的学习体验。

课堂形态分析超越对课堂的互动实践研究,从更加具有整体性的内容、活动和时空维度探索课堂的面貌,特别是借助课堂智能分析,开创非介入视角、规模化样本、多模态数据的课堂研究新局面,从而有助于拓展并深化当前的课堂研究。它预示着课堂研究新范式的诞生,必将为课堂转型路径的探索提供新的思路!

本文系全国教育科学规划2018年度教育部重点课题"指向立德树人的三科统编教材典型课例分析"(DEA180347)的部分成果。

注释

① 为便于讨论,本文对"范式"的理解遵循其提出者托马斯·库恩的经典认识:范式一方面代表着一个特定共同体的成员所共有的信念、价值、技术等构成的整体。另一方面指称那个整体的一种元素,即具体的谜题解答。参见:[美]托马斯·库恩.科学革命的结构[M].金吾伦,胡新和,译.北京:北京大学出版社,2003:157.

参考文献

[1][18][美]小威廉·E·多尔,等.混沌、复杂性、课程与文化:一场对话[M].余洁,译.北京:教育科学出版社,2014:导论;238.

[2][美]菲利普·W·杰克逊.课堂生活[M].丁道勇,译.北京:北京师范大学出版社,2001:221.

[3][5][日]佐藤学.课程与教师[M].钟启泉,译.北京:教育科学出版社,2003:344;218.

[4] Doyle, W. Paradigms in Teacher Effectiveness Research [J], Review of Research on Teacher Effectiveness. 1975,5(1):163-198.

[6] Eisenhart, M. (2001). Changing conceptions of culture and ethnographic methodology: recent thematic shifts and their implications for research and teaching [A], in Richardson, V. (Ed.) (2001). Handbook of research on teaching(Fourth Edition) [C]. Washington, DC: American Educational Research Association. P.209.

[7] 王鉴.课堂研究概论[M].北京:人民教育出版社,2007,43.

[8] 钟启泉.课堂研究[M].上海:华东师范大学出版社,2016.

[9] Hill, H., Kapitula, L. & Umland, K. (2011). A Validity Argument Approach to Evaluating Teacher Value-Added Scores[J]. American Educational Research Journal, 48(3):794-831.

[10] Little, O., L. Goe and C. Bell(2009). A practical guide to evaluating teacher effectiveness [R]. National Comprehensive Center for Teacher Quality, Washington, DC.

[11][13][14][31] OECD. Global Teaching InSights: A Video Study of Teaching [EB/OL], OECD Publishing, Paris. https://doi.org/10.1787/20d6f36b-en, 2020-11-30/2022-8-29.

[12] Clarke, D., Emanuelsson, J., Jablonka, E. & Mok, I.A.C.. The learner's Perspective Study and International Comparisons of Classroom Practice [A], in Clarke, D., Emanuelsson, J., Jablonka, E. & Mok, I. A. C. (eds.) (2006). Making Connections: Comparing Mathematics Classrooms Around the World [C]. Rotterdam: Sense Publishers, Pp.1-22.

[15] 杨晓哲.基于人工智能的课堂分析架构:一种智能的课堂教学研究[J].全球教育展望,2021,50(12):55-65.

[16] 张春雷.核心素养视角下课堂结构的审视与重构[J].教师教育研究,2018,30(5):66-71.

[17] 吴南中,夏海鹰,黄娥.课堂形态演进:迈向大数据支持的大规模个性化教学[J].电化教育研究.2020(9):81-87.

[19][30] [美]戴维·H·乔纳森,苏珊·M·兰德.学习环境的理论基础[M].徐世猛,李洁,周小勇,译.上海:华东师范大学出版社,2002:2;14-15.

[20] Young, M. & Lambert, D. Knowledge and the Future School [J]. London: Bloomsbury, 2014,74-76.

[21][27] [美]格兰特·威金斯,杰伊·麦克泰格.追求理解的教学设计(第二版)[M].闫寒冰,译.上海:华东师范大学出版社,2017:75.

[22][36] [美]戴维·索恩伯格.学习场景的革命[M].徐烨华,译.杭州:浙江教育出版社,2020:8.

[23] 吴刚平.知识分类视野下的记中学、做中学与悟中学[J].全球教育展望.2013,42(6):10-17.

[24] OECD. When Practice Meets Policy in Mathematics Education: A 19 Country/Jurisdiction Case Study [EB/OL]. https://www.oecd-ilibrary.org/education/when-practice-meets-policy-in-mathematics-education_07d0eb7d-en, 2020-08-20/2022-03-04.

[25] Erickson H.L., Lanning, L. A., & French, R. (2017). Concept-Based Curriculum and Instruction for the Thinking Classroom(2nd Edition), Thousand Oaks, CA: Corwin.

[26] 刘徽.概念地图:以大概念促进深度学习[J].教育发展研究.2021,41(24):53-63.

[28] 崔允漷.学科实践,让"自主、合作、探究"迭代升级[EB/OL].www.moe.gov.cn/fbh/live/2022/54382/zjwz/202204/t20220421_620105.html.2022-04-21/2022-4-27.

[29] R·基思·索耶.剑桥学习科学手册(第2版)[M].徐晓东,等译.北京:教育科学出版社,2021:709.

[32][33] Duncheon, J. & Tierney, W. G. (2013). Changing Conceptions of Time: Implications for Educational Research and Practice [J]. Review of Educational Research,83(2):236-272.

[34][35] [美]詹姆斯·贝兰卡,罗恩·勃兰特.21世纪学习的愿景[M].安桂清,主译.上海:华东师范大学出版社,2020:85.

Science Education in the Age of Misinformation

Professor Jonathan Osborne

Graduate School of Education, Stanford University

Abstract

An essential challenge we face today is we are living in a post-truth society — a society where facts have less value or less respect than they used to have and where expertise has also been challenged by the advent of the internet. At the same time, students are not so much digital natives as digital novices. Science education needs to provide students with an understanding of the social practices of science, because this is the knowledge the competent outsider needs to make judgment about whether the knowledge or claims they are reading have been vetted and put through that particular process, and how science functions as a community. Therefore, science education needs to put more emphasis on the basic techniques of digital media literacy, which should be a core feature of every discipline.

Keywords: science education; credibility of information; digital novice; epistemology; misinformation; post-truth society

My talk will address science education in an age of misinformation. The first question you might ask about this is "Why does this matter?" "Why is this needed?" or "What has this particularly got to do with science?" You can find many of the answers in the full version of our recently published report in *Science*, where we give a lengthy and hopefully really readable summary of what the arguments are for.

But prior to that, with the rise of what you might call a flood or tide of misinformation that has come with the arrival of Web 2.0, it is an issue that I think previous versions and iterations of school science standards failed to consider or address. I think it leads to the realization that there has been a fundamental change in the context in which we now live, the way in which society has to respond, and the way in which science education in particular has a duty to meet some of the challenges.

What are the challenges? The essential challenge is that we are now living in what has been characterized as a post-truth society. That is a society where facts have less value or less respect than they used to have and where expertise has also been challenged by the advent of the internet. Because people think "Why do I need an expert when I get all the information for myself and I evaluate myself?" For me, I think this is a profound fallacy. Nevertheless, this type of thinking is out there and it has led to lots of people believing in things that are challenging in that kind of way.

The kinds of challenges you're confronted with are these kinds of things, particularly with Covid-19, where there have been many claims about the value of masks, about things like hydrometer or about the hydropox chloroprene. And the challenge for the individual is "Are these claims to be believed, and how do you make that decision, or can I make that decision in that kind of way?"

Do I think, while this one question can be a temporary challenge, is a climate change an anthropogenic effect? I suspect most of you will think of it as a silly question. We knew the answer that it clearly is. But the more interesting question is why do you believe that? And I think the question of why you believe that is essentially interesting. The answer is twofold: we believe it because we recognize that it is a consensus of experts, and we have trust in experts, or we believe it because it is reported in media that we trust as well. The fundamental issue is how we decide whom to trust, particularly which scientific experts we are going to trust. Because what we are confronted with is a society that otherwise has been labeled a society of truth decay, where facts are of diminishing value and there is a disregard for the expertise. It is a challenge to society when people act on information that is fundamentally flawed. True knowledge in that sense is a collective good and it's important that people can understand and work out what is true and distinguish it from what is false.

This is a report consisting of a group of scientists or science educators. Carl Bergstrom is a scientist; Saul Perlmutter is a Nobel Prize winner; Anastasia Kozyreva is a psychologist. In addition, there are scholars, such as Sam Weinberg, who conduct research on civic scientific reasoning. We met over the course of about 6 months in 2021 and we developed and wrote this report; we now have it out there and it is a subject of an article which is coming out in *Science* this week on October 27th, 2022. It is based on publications by Dietmar Hotecke and Douglas Allchin on reconceptualizing nature of science education in the age of social media, by Clark Chin and Sarit Barzilai on education for a post truth world, and by Anastasia Kozyreva on citizens versus the Internet.

I said that true knowledge is a collective good, now there is no doubt about it when it comes to the Internet. There are things that are particularly valuable about the Internet —

wonderful for looking up answers to all kinds of questions we have. But there is a lot of misinformation — people are promoting ideas which essentially are fundamentally scientifically flawed. The earth is flat being a classic one. Or the ivermectin can cure you or prevent you from getting COVID-19, that the moon landing was a hoax, that masks are ineffective in preventing the spread of COVID-19, or climate change is not anthropogenic — that is just a sample of some of the misinformation. And the issue is how science education should respond to this, if at all?

This leads to the four questions in our report. The first question is "Why do students need the ability to evaluate expertise and information?" The second question is "What evidence is there that young people struggle?" The third question is "Why is it an urgent priority for scientists and science educators to develop students' competencies to evaluate information?" And then the fourth question: "What can be done by scientists and science educators to develop a competency to evaluate scientific information?"

Those are our four questions and what I'm going to try and run through briefly is the answers. Let's start with the first question. Why is this competence needed? First of all, the Internet is a novel information environment, although you may not think so: You might think it's been around for a long period of time, but the reality is it has only been around for 20 years and has had a profound effect on our society. Web 2.0 and the ability for people to generate their own websites and promote their own information has really only grown in the last 10 years. What we have seen in the last 10 years is that the maelstrom of misinformation is a threat. It is a threat because there are very few gatekeepers on the Internet: Anybody can publish what they like and anybody can circulate it and people will recirculate it. And, as somebody famously said, a false can be halfway around the world before the truth has even gotten its boots on.

People think that young people are digital natives, but young people are not so much digital natives as digital novices. What's my evidence? This is some research done by my colleague Sam Weinberg at Stanford. And he writes there, "As researchers have shown, such claims persist despite a 2019 national survey of 3 446 high school students that revealed major deficiencies in evaluating the credibility of online sources." These are the claims that they are competent. In addition, 52%, for instance, said that a Facebook video claiming to show ballot stuffing during the 2016 Democratic primary elections, a video that came from Russia, are fat, easily established by searching for 2006 voter fraud video, constituted strong evidence of US voter fraud. Clearly, they don't have the competency, the capability or the knowledge about how to effectively evaluate information.

Science education across the globe is based on a premise that it can prepare students to be scientifically literate — it cannot, because basically, students can never have sufficient scientific knowledge to deal with the science that they're confronted with today, much of which is not in the science curriculum, let alone the science which is to come. Basically, we are all put into a position of evaluating scientific expertise and making a judgment about who to trust — we are essentially epistemically dependent.

Science educators need to recognize that we need to prepare people or give them competency to make judgments about scientific expertise. These are what I think are the implications for science education. The students may be digital natives, but they are fundamentally digital novices. Just like people need to be taught and shown how to read in a sophisticated manner, they need to be taught and shown how to evaluate information on the Internet in a sophisticated manner.

The key issue is trust and credibility and that means you need to educate people about the basic criteria for trust and credibility. There are obviously more sophisticated versions of this, but just the basics would help people or inoculate them against much of this misinformation. We have to reframe and think about what we're educating people to become. We're not so much educating them to become scientifically literate in the delusion that they can become intellectually independent while educating them to be competent outsiders. What kinds of competencies are required as a competent outsider? That's really what the substance of our report is about.

I think the first question is "What can be done?" There is not much digital literacy here. This is the responsibility of all school subjects, not just science. In order to do that, we need to draw on the knowledge and expertise of experts. And the experts in this case are the fact-checkers. What do experts do when confronted with information claims on the Internet? They use an important strategy called click restraint. They recognize that when they put a question into Google, much of what they get at the top is either an advertisement or what has been selected for them on the basis of an algorithm. They do not read the top one, which is what our students do intend to do. Experts look through the list and look for the one which might be the most appropriate. One of the things experts also do, and I suspect many of you are not aware of: there are three little dots beside each source, if you press on that, it tells you something about the source. Then they choose one to open and when they land on that one, they actually don't spend that long there, because the first question they're asking is "Who is the person behind this website or who is the institution behind this website?" I will check them out first of all.

Within 30 seconds they often leave the website; they open another tab and they use that as a process called lateral reading. To ask questions about the source, they use Wikipedia or snopes.com or sourcewatch.org. We've summarized this as a three-stage process, as a simple heuristic. You have to ask, "Is the source of information credible? Is there conflict of interest? Is there an ideological bias? Is there political neutrality or other signs of objectivity?" If the answer is yes to any of those, then you should think about rejecting the source. If it passes those tests, you then go on to the second test, that is, "Does the source have the expertise to vouch for the claim? What is their evidence that they have a track record in the field? Do they have a reputation amongst their peers? What are their credentials or experience, and what's the institutional context from which they come?"

These are the basics of digital media literacy. The point at which scientific knowledge comes in is you need to have some understanding of how expertise is defined in science to answer that second question. How do you answer those particular questions in the context of science? You've got answers for those in the context of a car mechanic, or you've got answers for those in the context of a plumber. What are the same things in science?

Why is it important, then, for science in particular to address this? You might think civics can do the same thing. I disagree, because there are things that can only be done in science, and you have to start from the recognition that science occupies the epistemic high ground. By that I don't mean that there's something privileged about scientific knowledge; what I mean is that they are the purveyors of misinformation. The second thing is that all of us lack the knowledge to evaluate the data and evidence themselves. I could not evaluate the data and evidence on climate change; I do not have the expertise. In a sense, our knowledge is bounded. We know a lot about a very narrow area in that sense — we are an outsider to all other areas.

Producing reliable knowledge is a core commitment to science — the goal of science. The question is: how does it achieve that? It achieves that by aiming for consensus. Science puts a premium on the intersubjective agreement. Once science achieved that, it moves on, and therefore scientific consensus is fundamentally very important in the context of science. It achieves this by using an extensive process of peer review, not just on any one publication, but on funding, on pre-paper print. The whole community is a critical community devoted to finding out if there are flaws: if there are no flaws, that means it survives.

There are criteria for scientific expertise. What are those particular criteria? Obviously, in some senses, it is whom you work for; it is your PhD; it is what field you work in and where you put your publications. In some senses it is also prize-winning, but a Nobel Prize winner in physics does not make you an expert in evolutionary biology. These kinds of things need to be explained to students.

Students also need some knowledge of uncertainty; that is fundamentally important. Science does not produce certain knowledge. You need to be able to explain, for instance, why we cannot forecast the weather in two weeks' time accurately. You need some understanding of the distinction between cause and correlation, and you also need some understanding of how we as humans often make errors in reasoning. We suffer from particular things like confirmation bias — looking for evidence that match our views. This then takes us to the third step in our process, that is, there is a consensus among the relevant scientific experts. If there is, then it is wise to accept the consensus, as very rarely anybody stands against the consensus and is right. But one person often used by naysayers is Galileo, and he is an exception. If there is no consensus then you need to ask what is the nature of the agreement? What do the most highly regarded experts think? What range of findings are being delivered?

I think there is also a need to generate intellectual humility — you need to realize that what you are getting off the Internet is information. Knowledge is something different: knowledge is the ability to take that information and see its significance in a coherent framework. It is important to know how an entity or concept is related to others: what is significant, how it came to be and why this knowledge can be trusted. Knowing what photosynthesis is, for instance, is of little value by itself; what is valuable is being able to explain its significance, understand why it's such a crucial and important reaction and how it's sustained. And that is knowledge.

What we argue in the report is science education needs to provide an understanding of the social practices of science, because this is the knowledge the competent outsider needs to make judgment about whether the knowledge or claims they are reading have been vetted and put through that particular process, and how science functions as a community. Science education needs to put some emphasis on what you might call the basic techniques of digital media literacy, and that has to be a core feature of every discipline.

It is clearly something that should be addressed in the next iteration of Standards. We need new curriculum materials and the report gives some examples of those which I don't have time to present here, but I do urge you to have a look at some of the simple exercises that can be done. A program of professional development is also called for. That is necessary because most of us who teach science have never been practicing scientists. We do not understand the social practices of science ourselves. If you don't know something or don't understand it, it's very difficult to teach it. So professional development is required. Lastly, new assessments are needed. I am glad to say that the assessments in PISA 2025 will have a new competency to assess students' abilities to research and evaluate the credibility of scientific information. Changes in assessments are important because assessments are in some sense the levers which drive much of what people teach.

Related publications

Osborne, J., & Allchin, D. (2024). Science literacy in the twenty-first century: Informed trust and the competent outsider. *International Journal of Science Education*. https://doi.org/10.1080/09500693.2024.2331980.

Wilson, C. D. D., Haudek, K. C. C., Osborne, J. F. F., Buck Bracey, Z. E., Cheuk, T., Donovan, B. M. M., ... Zhai, X. (2023). Using automated analysis to assess middle school students' competence with scientific argumentation. *Journal of Research in Science Teaching*, 61(1), 38–69.

Osborne, J., & Pimentel, D. (2023). Science education in an age of misinformation. *Science Education*, 107(3), 553–571.

Osborne, J., & Pimentel, D. (2022). Science, misinformation, and the role of education. *Science*, 378(6617), 246–248. https://doi.org/10.1126/science.abq8093.

课堂教与学的革新

转轴拨弦三两声：探索中国课堂上的"回音"话语*

肖思汉

【摘要】如何研究和展现中国课堂的精致、精巧与精妙？本文以"回音"为例，探索一种基于细致描述和理论阐释的取径。通过对上海市某初中一位资深教师的生命科学课堂上的三个"回音"片段进行话语分析，本文呈现了三种难以归类的"回音"话语，它们既在结构或功能上神似奥康纳和迈克尔斯及其追随者所研究的话语，又与其有着丰富而细微的差别。从这些"回音"话语中，可以看到中国教师独特的教学智慧。借助这些分析，本文进而讨论了中国课堂研究者如何面对和处理舶来的概念和理论的问题。

【关键词】课堂互动；回音；话语分析；质性方法论

【作者简介】肖思汉/华东师范大学课程与教学研究所副教授

Tuning the Pegs and Testing the String: The Discourse Practice of Revoicing in a Classroom in China

XIAO Sihan

(Institute of Curriculum and Instruction, East China Normal University, Shanghai, 200062)

Abstract: How to (re-) present the ingenuity of teaching and learning in the classroom in China? This article aims to illustrate an approach that is based upon detailed description and interpretation with theories, using the discourse practice of revoicing as an example. In particular, I present discourse analyses on three episodes from a middle school life sciences classroom where an experienced teacher deployed revoicing techniques that were, to some extent, similar to what O'Connor and Michaels and their followers documented, yet had nuanced and profound variances. I argue that these variances show great ingenuity of Chinese teachers against the backdrop of cultural beliefs and practice in China's schools. I also discuss

---

* 致谢：本文的思路是在多次讲座和研讨会的基础上———更准确地说，是在与同行的多次互动中———形成和发展的。为此，我要感谢北京师范大学教师教育研究中心、重庆市教育科学研究院、上海市浦东教育发展研究院、上海市延安初级中学等单位的同行，以及（尤其是）"空间站"的伙伴们。

the methodological concerns of using Western concepts and theories in looking closely into classrooms in China.

Keywords: classroom interaction; revoicing; discourse analysis; qualitative research methodology

一、引言

在《如何呈现一场课堂互动》一文的结尾,我写道:我国的课堂研究者应该"尽最大努力呈现出中国课堂的复杂性,并通过多样、深入、富有理论的分析,展现出中国课堂'枝蔓丛生'的精致、精巧与精妙"[1]。近两年来,有一些同行向我抛来这个问题:什么叫"枝蔓丛生",该如何展现?

本文以"回音"为例,呈现我对这个问题的初步探索。作为课堂话语研究的经典之作,美国学者奥康纳(M. C. O'Connor)和迈克尔斯(S. Michaels)的"回音"(revoicing)概念得到了一代代研究者的不断引用和发展。但是,中国课堂上的"回音"是什么样子?与国外有何区别?这些问题学界鲜有涉足。另一方面,得益于华东师范大学教研员研修中心这一平台,近年来,我有机会与来自全国各地的中小学教师、教研员、校长一起交流课堂研究的成果与方法,其间常常用到一个美国小学科学课堂的"回音"案例[2]。在惊叹于这一话语之妙的同时,有些教师产生了这样的疑惑:我们中国的课堂上难道没有这样的话语吗?还有一些教师则质疑:这样的互动当然很好,但我们课时这么紧张,班额又这么大,还有考试的压力,我们心有余而力不足呀!正是在学术与实践的双重追问下,我想借由此文,就以上问题求教于方家。

二、"回音"的经典研究及其延续

什么是"回音"?让我们先来看一个示例(见表1)。

表1 "回音"示例

01		教师:	你是怎么得出这个数字的?
02		小灰:	我就是把它的长度加上宽度,然后乘以二。
03	→	教师:	所以你不同意小黑的观点,你的意思是不用把四条边的长度都量出来,是吗?
04		小灰:	是的。

这段对话一共有四个话轮。在第一话轮,教师提出了一个问题(01)。在第二话轮,学生小灰做出了一个回应(02)。在常规的师生对话中,教师在第三话轮应该评价小灰的回答(例如"很对,请坐"或"不对,还有其他意见吗")。然而,教师此时并没有做出评价,而是重新组织语言,转述了小灰的回应,并询问小灰是否同意自己的转述。在第四话轮,小灰认可了教师的转述。奥康纳和迈克尔斯将教师的第三话轮称为"回音"。

这两位学者在两篇开拓性的论文中阐述了"回音"的结构和功能。[3][4]首先,在结构上,"回音"通常含有一个表示合理推断的语言标记。例如,在以上示例中,教师的"所以"和"你的意思是"都表示,接下来她要说的话,是在对小灰之前的回应做出合理的推断(而不是自己的新观点)。其次,"回音"的主体通常是一个间接引语,它进一步表明教师是在转述,而不是在做新的陈述,这个间接引语通常会对第二话轮的语义进行某种重新组织,从而达到某种修辞的目的。最后,"回音"通常以一个附加问句结尾,从而为学生创造出第四话轮,此时,学生有权利评价教师对自己观点的转述是否正确,在课堂上掌握了更多的话语权。至于"回音"的功能,奥康纳和迈克尔斯提到了很多种情况,例如澄清学生的观点、引入术语、引导教学进程、将学生的声音扩大传播给全班等等。但她们着重分析的,主要是两个功能:一是重构学生和知识之间的关系,让学生对某个更准确、更学科化,或者在当下更关键的观点拥有所有权(如示例中的"不用把四条边的长度都量出来");二是重构学生和学生之间的关系,赋予他们社会角色,制造观点上的同盟或对立(如示例中的小灰和小黑)。

在奥康纳和迈克尔斯的经典研究之后,"回音"这一课堂话语引起了教育学界的广泛关注和深入探索。不同国家的学者们开始在自己的语言、社会、文化情境里研究这一话语现象。其中,有些研究提出了新的概念或术语,但其内核依然是经典的"回音"结构,其功能也大同小异。例如,麦克尼尔(L. McNeil)等人把回音分为三个类型:重复、阐述和转述。[5]巴(Bae)等人提出了"软支架"的概念,其中包括回音、转向、浮显、拓展等具体策略。[6]埃涅迪(Enyedy)等学者在双语(英语、西班牙语)教学的数学课堂上发现,教师的回音具有七种功能:将发言的学生与其他学生对立起来;检验和评价学生的回答正确与否;引导学生遵循课堂规则;凸显学生对于当前数学任务的贡献;强调当前的学习目标;发展学生的数学身份认同;为英语的正确使用作出示范。其中,评价回答的正确性、引导学生遵循规则和凸显学生的贡献是这位教师所用回音的主要功能。[7]弗勒德(Flood)提出了"多模态回音"(multimodal revoicing)的概念。她从维果茨基(L. Vygotsky)关于"日常概念"和"科学概念"的理论区分出发,运用常人方法学的交谈分析方法,展示了用手势进行回音是如何帮助学习者在具身的日常经验和更学科性的科学概念之间建立关联的。[8]与此类似,阿利巴利(Alibali)等人通过三个案例,展示了数学教师是如何通过手势对学生的观点进行回音的。他们认为,教师的手势可以让学生观点里模糊、含混、指代不清的地方变得更加清晰、精确。[9]

大多数关于"回音"的研究都是在英语国家进行的,关注的是以英语为主要语言的课堂(有少数研究是在双语课堂上关注双语教学中的"回音"),只有极少数的研究关注其他语言的"回音"话语,而关注中国课堂的研究则更为少见。一些中国课堂话语研究者在分析中提及了"回音",虽然分析本身十分精彩,但"回音"话语本身并不是他们研究的焦点。[10][11][12]郁志珍和秦乐琦的学位论文都深入研究了中国课堂上的"回音"话语。基于福曼(Forman)等人的概念框架,郁志珍将她所研究的小学科学课堂上的"回音"分为重复、改述、扩展和宣告四类,并提炼出关联教学内容、操纵学生观点立场、诱发学生进一步回应等功能。[13]秦乐琦通过更为细致的分析,将我国小学数学课堂上的"回音"分为归纳式、征询式和评价式三类,且每一类下分别有三种具体的话语策略。[14]最近,任冰尔和孙丽丽将中国课堂上的"回音"分为试探式、转播式、探索式和开放式四类,分别起到信息重组、静态评价、动态推进和多向互动的功能。[15]总的来说,虽然上述三项研究都对中国课堂上的"回音"做了规范、系统化的数据采集与分析,但它们都有一种"结构化"的倾向,关心的更多是如何给案例分类,而缺少对每一个案例更为细致的解读。这样做虽然让我们得以看到中国课堂"回音"的宏观样貌,给读者以很大的启发,但在结构的背后,这些"回音"和国外课堂上的"回音"究竟有何种差别,依然难以分辨。

较之以上文献,沈(Sum)和权(Kwon)对韩国课堂的研究与本文"非结构化"的阐释主义倾向更为相近。这两位研究者基于韩国的儒家文化背景———尤其是"敬语"语言体系———探索一位资深教师在数学课堂上运用回音的方式。作者认为,与英语课堂上的回音相比,韩国课堂上的回音有几个差异:第一,在转述学生的话语时,教师需注意敬语的变换,并往往用巧妙的方式消解了这些敬语;第二,韩国课堂是集体主义的,具有一种群体导向的世界观(例如学生普遍习惯于齐声应答),所以教师必须把学生作为群体中的一员来处理,而不是作为个人来处理;第三,个人的观点和论辩也是属于整个群体的,那些用"我"开头的陈述,实际上也在代表"我们";第四,学生更愿意服从群体的想法,所以数学知识更容易被视为是群体或班级所共同建构的。[16]值得注意的是,作者并未急于给他们所观察到的"回音"分类或命名,而是更多地以描述的姿态,记录这位教师"回音"的种种特征。

在本文中,我运用话语分析的方法探索中国课堂上的三个回音片段。不同于郁志珍等人的做法,我不打算(也不能够)为"回音"分类。我想做的是尽可能细致地描述我所看到的课堂,并分析"话语何以发生"。我想通过这样的分析说明两点:中国课堂上存在"回音"这一话语;但是,就这三个片段而言,它们与已有文献中的"回音"都不一样,有着细微的差别。和《如何呈现一场课堂互动》中的案例一样,本文的三个片段都来自上海市某初中的李老师(数据采集时的教龄为21年)所任教的生命科学课堂。对于每一个片段,我会首先简要描述其教学背景和情境,呈现其转录文本,然后对话语进行分析。我的分析主要聚焦的问题是:李老师是怎样进行回音的?在随后的讨论部分,我会转而探讨以下问题:这些回音与已有文献有何区别?这样的分析意味着什么?

三、"着凉了会感冒":在转述与纠正之间

第一个片段来自2017年5月17日的一节课,教学内容是沪教版《生命科学》八年级下册的"生物的类群"一章的"微生物"一节。李老师在前一节课让学生集体观看了一段关于人经历感冒全过程的视频。在本节课上,李老师组织学生们一起讨论这段视频,探究感冒是怎样发生的。在讨论的过程中,有一位女生提出了困惑:"这个片子里说感冒都是因为有病毒,那为什么

我们会说着凉了然后感冒了呢?"李老师认为这是一个"很好的问题",并对女生的观点进行了回音:"她说,不是片子告诉我们,生病的原因是有病毒进入体内吗?那怎么着凉了会感冒呢?是不是?"随后,他转向全班,问道:"你们同意着凉了会感冒吗?"接下来,有一位男生表达了他的观点,并与李老师发生了一段对话,如表2所示。

表2 "着凉了会感冒"片段转录文本

01		男生一:	着凉了会感冒?
02		李老师:	(望向该男生)同意吗?
03		男生一:	不同意。
04		李老师:	为什么不同意?
05		男生一:	因为我没怎么感冒过。
06	→	李老师:	就是着凉以后没怎么感冒过。
07		男生一:	着凉之后没感冒过。
08	→	李老师:	他的意思就是,我着凉了,但我并不一定感冒,而且很多时候不会感冒,是这个意思吗?
09			
10			(男生一点头。)

这位男生首先抛出了一个反问(01),李老师确认其态度(02),得到了男生明确的回应:他不同意"着凉了会感冒"这一观点(03)。李老师进一步要求他为自己的观点提供理由(04)。男生第一次提供的理由,从字面意义本身来说,是不够贴切的,因为"我没怎么感冒过"(05)是一个宽泛的描述,和"着凉"并没有直接的关系。李老师的下一个话轮以"就是"开头,这可以被视为"也就是说"的缩略,是一个表示合理推断的语言标记,亦即,李老师的这句话是一个回音(06)。这个回音看似是在重复男生的观点,但多了一个元素:"着凉以后"。这一说法补上了"着凉"和"感冒"的时间关系,使其成为了一个可以用来反驳原观点的论据,即:我不同意着凉了会感冒,因为我着凉以后没怎么感冒过。男生肯定了教师这一纠正后的说法(07)。不过,从科学论辩的角度来看,这个论证依然有两个缺陷:第一,就证据类型而言,属于个人经验,科学性不强;第二,就语气而言,过于肯定和绝对,没有为可能的反驳留下进一步论辩的空间。已有研究表明,模糊而留有余地的语气是科学论证话语的显著特点。[17]

李老师接下来的一次回音再一次帮助男生做出了纠正(08—09)。这一回音至少有五个细节值得我们注意。第一,李老师首先说"他的意思就是",明确了这位男生对观点的所有权(而不是自己在评价或修改他的观点)。第二,李老师用"我并不一定感冒"这一新的说法,在男生观点的基础上引入了概率,从而弱化了原观点的绝对性,做出了让步,"着凉后并不一定会感冒"的论证力度比"我着凉之后没感冒过"要强,更能抵御反驳。第三,"而且很多时候不会感冒"是在"不一定会感冒"的基础上,偏向于原观点的"不会感冒",这一补充又部分地支持了原观点。第四,虽然李老师的回音里依然有"我",但相比男生的原观点(05,07),这一说法淡化了个人经验的成分,更能被视为一种普遍化的陈述(例如,把李老师回音中的两个"我"分别换成

"某个人"和"这个人",一样念得通)。第五,李老师最后用"是这个意思吗"这一附加问句,与"他的意思就是"呼应,重新界定了这个观点的所有权,并创造了下一个话轮,把评价的权利还给了男生。随后,男生点头,对李老师的"重复"表示了认可(10)。

在这个片段中,李老师的话语到底是传统的"引发—回应—评价"(IRE),还是"回音",似乎很难说。一方面,他的话语在结构上确实具备"回音"的要素,而且看起来确实是在转述。另一方面,比较转述与原观点的不同之处,李老师加以调整的地方,又恰恰是男生观点的错漏之处,这种精确的改动,又起到了纠正的作用,而不仅仅是思维的引导和推进。我认为,这是一种介于转述和纠正之间的独特"回音"。

四、"老板,你要不要":剧场和角色的营造

第二个片段来自于2017年3月9日的一节课,教学内容是沪教版《生命科学》八年级下册的"生物的类群"一章的"生物的分类"一节。为了让学生理解林奈(C. von Linné)双名命名法的由来,李老师设计了一个情境,让学生讨论不同语言和方言的人对"红薯"这种食物的不同叫法,然后问道:"在日常生活中,对同一样事物的叫法不同,尚且还行得通,但在科学上,必须有精确的命名,让全球不同语言的人都能有效沟通,应该怎样命名才好呢?"有些学生立即提议,可以用英文,因为"大部分国家(的人)都会学习英文",所以"大家多少都会知道一些"。但这个提议遭到了另一些学生的否定,他们认为并非所有国家的人都会英文,或者能熟练使用英文。正在课堂陷入短暂沉默的时候,有一位男生提出了他的想法,如表3所示。

表3 "老板,你要不要"片段转录文本

01		(男生三小声说话。)
02	李老师:	嗯?
03	男生三:	使用数字编号。
04	李老师:	用数字编号,怎么编码?
05	男生四:	世界上那么多东西……
06	女生二:	这么多……
07		(还有其他学生小声议论。)
08 →	李老师:	好,也就是说,每一种生物都像有一个手机号一样,对不对?
09	男生三:	Yes。
10 →	李老师:	所以,老板,我有一串110120119,然后想卖给你,你要不要?
11		(众学生笑。)
12	某男生:	我不要。
13 →	李老师:	我另外还有一串110119119119120,你要不要?
14		(众学生笑。)

在这个片段的开头,男生三提出了"使用数字编号"的主张(03)。李老师首先复述了他的观点,随即提出了一个问题:"怎么编码?"(04)在这个问题的提示下,不少学生都对这一主张提出了疑义(05—07)。例如,男生四的回应("世界上那么多东西")虽然不是一个完整的表述,但

我们可以推测其意思是:世界上有那么多东西,用数字编号怎么编得过来?

对于此时课堂上出现的质疑,李老师似乎没有理会,他用"好"肯定了男生三的发言(08)。他接下来的一句具备"也就是说"这一表示合理推断的语言标记,也具备"对不对"这一附加问句,从语言形式上看,完全符合回音的结构。然而,"每一种生物都像有一个手机号一样"和男生三之前的"使用数字编号"看似没有意义上的直接关联,很难说是一种内容的转述。即使从语境来看,我们能够理解这两句话的联系,从而将其视为回音,但这一回音的用意何在?男生三对李老师的回音给予了肯定回应(09)。此外,值得留意的是,这个英文的"yes"透露出课堂上的气氛是比较随意的,学生和李老师的关系是比较亲近的。

紧接着,李老师说道:"所以,老板,我有一串110120119,然后想卖给你,你要不要?"(10)这是一个非常特殊的回音形式。一方面,跟上一个回音一样,它也有"所以"这个表示合理推断的语言标记,并以一个附加问句收尾("你要不要")。但另一方面,这一回音有几个和已有研究不一样的特征。第一,包裹在"所以"和"你要不要"之间的不是一个间接引语,而是一个直接引语(我们完全可以把中间的内容加上双引号)。第二,这个直接引语以"老板"这一身份称谓开头,它标记了一个重要的情境营造与转化,它和课堂情境里的常见称谓(如"老师""家长""校长"等)相隔太远,以至于一旦出现,所有参与者都知道接下来的话语将是一种暂时脱离于课堂情境之外的"剧本"。也就是说,"老板"构成了一个冈佩尔茨(Gumperz)所说的"情境化线索",帮助互动参与者理解接下来将要发生什么。[18]就这个片段来说,"老板"营造的是一个买卖的情境,李老师扮演的是卖家的角色,要把某个商品卖给买家。第三,中间这句直接引语既不是对男生三观点的转述,也不是进一步的解释说明,更不妨说是这个剧本中的一句台词。"我有一串110120119"是在把男生三的观点("使用数字编号")表演出来,而这样的表演给男生三的观点加上了一层荒谬的色彩。尤其是,"110120119"并不是一串随机的、无特定意义的数字,而是由所有人都熟知的三个急救电话号码组成的。从巴赫金(Bakhtin)的文本理论来看,李老师是在引用一个更大的社会话语[19]。这样的引用及其排列组合的形式,进一步增强了这句台词的荒谬性。从李老师说完这句话之后很多学生的笑声可以看出,课堂参与者都理解了这一表演,并被其荒谬逗笑了。第四,这一回音确实以附加问句结尾,但和经典的回音结构不同,李老师并非用"是不是""对不对"等形式询问学生对转述是否准确的意见,从而把评价的权利还给学生,而是停留在买卖的情境里,用"你要不要"将这场表演中的另一个角色——买家("老板")——赋予了学生;换言之,这个附加问句激活了学生的角色扮演。随后,当课堂上的某位男生回答"我不要"(12)的时候,这个回应有了两层含义:表面上,这是以买家的口吻表示"我不要买这串110120119",但实际上,这也是以学生的口吻表示"我不同意使用数字编号的提议"。也就是说,这个回应既是剧本的一部分、表演的一部分,同时也是课堂情境中针对正在讨论的问题的态度性回应。随后,李老师又再次回音,用一个形式相同但更加冗长的数字编码("110119119119120"),将这场表演的荒谬性表达得更为明显(13)。这个回音同样得到了全班学生的笑声回应(14)。

现在,回过头来,我们就能够理解李老师在这个片段中第一次回音的用意(08)。"每一种生物都像有一个手机号一样"从字面意义上看似与男生三的观点没有直接的关联,是一种过度的演绎,但它为李老师接下来的两次回音做了铺垫。从第一次回音,到第三次回音,李老师逐步营造出了一个临时的剧场,并把自己和学生置入其中,赋予了与课堂情境迥异的角色和剧本。

五、"多读鲁迅小说":教学与狂欢的平行时空

第三个片段来自于 2017 年 3 月 23 日的一节课,教学内容是沪教版《生命科学》八年级上册的"健康与疾病"一章的"认识健康"一节。《如何呈现一场课堂互动》一文呈现了这个片段的完整转录文本。此处,我们将聚焦该片段的开头部分,李老师向全班发问,如何让自己处于健康的状态。多位学生以自由回答的形式,提出自己的见解。这个时长 90 秒钟的片段如表 4 所示。

表 4 "多读鲁迅小说"片段转录文本(基于杰弗森转录规则)

01	李老师:	身体健康,我们可以做些什么?(1.0)我们做些什么,可以让
02		我们自己维持在身体健康的状态下?或者不够健康的,我们
03		恢复到健康状态下?
04		(3.0)
05		心理健康,我们可以做些什么,让自己处于一种比较良好的心
06		理健康状态下?
07	学生一:	多看一些对我们身体有益的东西。
08	李老师:	多看一些对身体有益的[东西,能具体说吗?
09	众生:	[呵呵呵呵呵,
10		(2.0)
11	李老师:	多看课文。
12		(2.5)
13	学生二:	鲁迅小说。=
14	众生:	=哈哈哈哈哈哈哈哈。
15 →	李老师:	多读[鲁迅小说对健康有益,=
16	众生:	[哈哈哈哈哈。
17	学生三:	=多读鲁迅。
18	众生:	哈哈哈哈哈。
19 →	李老师:	好。(1.5)除了读鲁迅能让自己健康以外,(众生捂嘴笑)我们
20		还可以做些什么,让自己尽可能多地保持在这样的状态下?
21		(2.0)
22	学生四:	多运动。
23	李老师:	多去运动,(1.5)对吧?多去什么样的运动,能具体吗?
24	学生四:	打篮球就是蛮好的。
25	李老师:	打篮球就是蛮好的。=

续 表

26	学生五：	=做瑜[伽。
27	李老师：	[你认为呢?
28		(3.0)
29	学生六：	°体能运动°。
30	李老师：	体能运动,就是力量运动,是吧,练练腹[肌的。
31	某学生：	[练练腹肌。
32	学生四：	素质训练。
33	众生：	呵呵[呵呵,
34	李老师：	[素质训练,有人说做瑜伽,素质运动。
35		(2.0)
36		好,还有吗?
37		(2.0)
38		身体健康、心理健康、社会适应性良好,我们可以做些什么?
39		(2.0)
40	→ 李老师：	我们现在有学生提到多去运动,多去::(1.0)阅读,特别是多读点鲁迅小说。
41		
42	某学生：	哈哈哈。(笑完后低头捂嘴,望向14行笑声最大的学生,但后者并未发笑,也并未望向前者。)
43		
44	李老师：	还有一些具体的运动,比如说有力量训练,做瑜伽,等等。(1.0)还有吗?
45		

在这个片段中,围绕"多读鲁迅小说",课堂上出现了数次哄堂大笑的时刻(09,14,16,18)。从正统的眼光来看,这是几位学生的故意捣乱所致,这样的玩笑对课堂秩序构成了干扰。不过,李老师并没有停下来对这样的哄堂大笑进行干预,更没有对捣乱的学生进行"管理"。相反,课堂上笑声最剧烈的一次,恰恰是在李老师提到"多读鲁迅小说"之后(16)。但是,在这次全班哄堂大笑后约45秒钟,李老师再次主动提到"多读点鲁迅小说"(40—41),课堂上几乎无人发笑了。如何理解这90秒钟的课堂?具体来说,如何理解李老师的话语?如何理解课堂上的笑与不笑?

可能有读者会说:"这还不简单吗?由于这是一个教师邀请学生集思广益、头脑风暴的情境,所以李老师选择了未加干预,不对课堂秩序进行管理,而是对学生的捣乱进行冷处理。这样做不会中断学生的发言。学生们最开始觉得这个玩笑很好笑,后来多说了几次,也就没那么好笑了,所以后来就不笑了。这是任何一个课堂上都有可能出现的、十分寻常普通的一个小插曲。"这么说固然有一定的道理。从李老师多次的停顿(04,12,21,28,35,37,39,45)可以看出,他确实是在期待更多的回应。所以,插科打诨或许是可以容忍和忽略的。但是,"冷处理"的说法无法解释为什么李老师自己会多次提到这一玩笑(15,19,40—41)。更关键的是,这个解释有些宏观,错过了这场互动的精妙之处。

片段伊始,当学生一说"多看一些对我们身体有益的东西"(07)时,玩笑已经开始,只是对我们这样的局外人来说,处于模糊不清的状态。当李老师重复该说法时,已经有许多学生开始发笑(09)。我们无从得知李老师作为局内人,此时是否已经领会了玩笑的用意。无论是否领会,李老师此时还是试图补全学生一的意思,所以在2秒钟的等待时间内,未能得到"能具体说吗"的回应,他便用试探的口吻说"多看课文"(11),但并没有学生接话。在2.5秒的沉默后,学生二接话说"鲁迅小说"(13),这句话立刻引发了全班的大笑。

李老师接下来的这句话值得仔细琢磨。尽管没有表示合理推断的语言标记,但从语义上看,这句话确实是对学生一和学生二的回答的转述。李老师在做的是,把"多看一些对我们身体有益的东西"和"鲁迅小说"结合在一起,形成了"多读鲁迅小说对健康有益"这一观点。并且,虽然句末没有附加问句,但李老师的语调上扬,依然是一种试探、问询的口吻,从而为第四话轮留出了余地。这样分析似乎已经足够,但我认为这个回音还有一层含义:它所指向的第二话轮除了学生一(07)和学生二(13)之外,还有全班的笑声(14)。此时,李老师不可能没有意识到这两位学生在开玩笑,而面对全班的哄堂大笑,李老师依然"一本正经"地合成并转述了他们的观点,所以他同时"回"给全班的,还有这个玩笑的成分。正是这样一句带着玩笑成分的回音,经由李老师这一权威之口说出,本身成为了玩笑的一部分,在那个瞬间创造出了巴赫金所说的"狂欢节"时刻[20],再次引发了全班更剧烈的笑声(16,18)。而之后的这些笑声,恰恰可以被视为第四话轮,是学生用集体大笑"肯定地评价"了李老师对这一玩笑的主动参与,"狂欢节"达到了高潮。

待笑声逐渐消退后,李老师说"好",再次开启话轮(19)。"除了读鲁迅能让自己健康以外"一句,起到两个作用。第一,顺着此前的"狂欢节",李老师把"多读鲁迅小说"确定为了一个合法的回应,(至少在表面上)没有否认学生一和学生二的贡献。第二,在确定合法性的同时,"除了……以外"的话语也明确地把这个玩笑置于一边,宣布"狂欢节"开始的人(15),也在此时宣告"狂欢节"结束(19)。何以见得这是一种宣告?我们固然无法探知李老师的意图,但从紧随其后的反应来看,此前肆无忌惮大笑的学生,此时只是捂嘴而笑,再也没有大声喧哗(15)。这一反应表明,对于互动参与者来说,这句话确实起到了"收场"的效果。在此之后,学生们回到正题,纷纷提出自己对于"如何维持健康状态"的看法。在一段密集的自由发言后,李老师用一个回音归纳学生们的意见(40—41)。此处,他再一次主动提到了"多读点鲁迅小说"。与之前不同的是,全班只有一位学生发出笑声;他的笑声剧烈但短暂,笑完迅速捂上了嘴,眼睛望向之前在"狂欢节"里笑得最大声的学生,而后者正在翻书,没有任何反应。这也再次印证,此刻大部分学生都已明白:"狂欢节"已经落幕了。

六、讨论

上文分析了李老师课堂上的三个"回音"片段。即使只比较这三个片段,我们也能发现,它们难以归类,有着丰富而细微的差别。这些"回音"有共同点吗?作为一个整体(如果可以暂且如此的话),它们和国外已有文献中的"回音"有什么区别?这样的分析又意味着什么?本节将尝试讨论这些问题。

(一) 知识与情感:发现中国教学智慧

在这三个片段中,李老师对学生回应的处理每每都神似奥康纳和迈克尔斯所界定的"回音",但又有一些不同之处。例如,在"着凉了会感冒"中,李老师本人的观点非常清晰地嵌于"回音"之中,使得他的话语介于转述和纠正之间。学生一方面对知识的建构有主动权和所有权,一方面又依然处于李老师的控制之下。又如,在"老板,你要不要"中,李老师的话语具有"回音"的基本结构,但在字面意义上完全摆脱了学生的原有观点,而营造出一个貌似与课堂无关的剧场,通过角色扮演完成了理答的过程。相反,在"多读鲁迅小说"中,通过结构精炼、时机精准的"回音",李老师加入学生的玩笑,创造出两个平行发展的时空———常规教学的时空,以及巴赫金意义上的"狂欢节"时空———从而不动声色地消解了学生的"捣乱"。

三个片段的共同之处(至少)在于,它们都显示出李老师在知识与情感,或者说效率与平等上达成的巧妙平衡。知识与情感的平衡在于,李老师的教学从来都不仅仅是为了知识的传授或能力的培养。如果仅为知识的传授,李老师完全可以采用传统的"引发—回应—评价"模式,让学生习得已经预设好的正确答案,或如经典的"回音"结构一样,通过转述学生的观点,不断重塑学生与知识、学生与学生之间的关系,从而将他们引入合作、沟通、创造与批判性思维的世界。但在三个片段中,李老师总是将课堂上的情感氛围、他与学生的社会关系也纳入教学之中,例如在"着凉了会感冒"中维系学生的面子,又如在"多读鲁迅小说"中维持课堂上的融洽氛围。效率与平等的平衡在于,尽管密集地使用"回音"话语,将课堂的主动权和知识的所有权"还给"学生,高度容忍学生的玩笑,甚至主动调侃,在剧场中"表演",但李老师的课堂依然推进迅速,有条不紊,在有限的课时中高效地完成教学任务,而不像国外许多"回音"弥漫的课堂,师生往往会长时间地讨论某个在我们眼中或许不值得浪费工夫的知识点。

这样的课堂互动显示出李老师所代表的中国教师的教学智慧。在中国的教育文化与实践中,知、情、意往往是统一而融通的,而不是分裂的;"做事"与"成人"往往是合二为一的。[21][22] 所以,相较于西方的教师,我国的教师会更加关注教学中的情感维度。埃里克森(Erickson)将学习定义为一种"同意的政治"———教学的达成,首先需要学生从情感上同意教师教自己,否则一切都是白搭。[23] 麦克德莫特(McDermott)指出,社会关系是学习的基础。[24] 李老师或许并不认识埃里克森和麦克德莫特,更不知道他们的理论,但这些道理早已深植在他的教学信念与实践之中。

(二) 寻找与透视:调整理论与实践的关系

或许有读者会产生这样的质疑:你口口声声说要"展现出中国课堂'枝蔓丛生'的精致、精巧与精妙",但你自己分析起中国课堂,引用的不依旧是奥康纳、迈克尔斯、巴赫金云云吗?这算什么"中国经验""中国故事"呢？实话实说，这个问题也困扰着我。最简单同时也看似坦诚的回应可能是：的确，这样的引用暴露出我对中国本土理论———尤其是中国哲学———了解之匮乏，应该多多补课，努力（只）用中国理论解释中国实践。可是，这样可能吗？这样就够了吗？我还没有答案。

不过，在想象我会如何与篇首提到的那些提出疑问的教师交流本文的时候，我产生了一些新的想法。从前，当我们看到一个类似于"回音"这样的概念的时候，我们的反应可能是：这个东西好！中国课堂上有吗？我们在中国的课堂上寻找一个舶来之物。如果有，皆大欢喜；如果没有，那么我们也要有。这种"寻找—补短"的模式往往给教师带来了短暂的兴奋和长久的困惑与疲惫。本文提出另一种"透视—取长"的模式。也就是说，虽然不需要避讳使用舶来的概念或理论，但我们并不是在中国课堂上寻找它们的踪迹，而是以它们为棱镜，透过它们来重新审视中国课堂，看见之前看不到或看不清的现象。通过"回音"的透视，我发现，李老师早就在不了解"回音"概念的情况下，熟练地运用这一话语，并且有着自己丰富的创造。他的话语实践，远远超出奥康纳和迈克尔斯的理论所涉猎的范围，体现出独特的中国智慧。我相信，透过其他的概念和理论，我们会看见更多样、更多彩的中国教育实践。

（三）套用与创造：概念转译中的裂隙与生机

在本文的写作过程中，我意识到"讲好中国教育故事"的另一重挑战，以及它所另辟的蹊径，那就是概念转译的问题。2016年与刘畅博士一起撰写《课堂话语如何影响学习———基于美国课堂话语实证研究的述评》一文时，我们在自己的写作中初次将"revoicing"译为"回音"。[25]我们当时采取的主要是直译的思路：将"re-"这一前缀译为"回"，将"voicing"译为"音"，而"回音"二字刚好本就是一个常见词汇，不会过于怪异或拗口。直到很久之后，我才发现这或许不是一个适切的译法，因为"revoicing"本身是一个动词的进行时形式，"revoice"是可以当动词使用的，而"回音"是一个名词。在中文里，我们可以说，甲"回答""回复"或"回应"了乙；在口语中，我们也可以简略地说，甲"回"了乙或者"你回她电话了吗"。但若说甲"回音"了乙，便很拗口，不是一种惯常的中文表达。我们的译法和原文之间是存在裂隙的。

但是，把概念从一种语言转译到另一种语言的过程，往往也是一个重新创造的过程（尽管作者当时可能是无意识的）。我现在才意识到，"回音"恰恰比"revoicing"更能贴合李老师的话语实践。因为"回音"本身就蕴含了两个声音：原本的声音，以及回响的声音。两种声音之间的关系，而不仅仅是其中某个声音，是这个中文概念传达的意义。正如李老师与学生之间的关系，始终是他的课堂上滋养着教学过程的一条潜流，无法忽视。更有意思的是，在关于"回音"的中文文献中，我看到了许多来自中小学教师的作品。这些作者完全没有引用奥康纳和迈克尔斯，他们丝毫不是在"revoicing"的意义上使用这个词。然而，"回音"在他们那里，恰恰是一个情感性、关系性的词汇，如"爱的回音"[26]、"心灵的回音"[27]、"感受的回音"[28]，等等。这种巧合的背后,是概念转译这项工作为理论本土化———或者说,在地理论发展———所带来的生机。

七、尾声

本文不是一篇完整的实证研究报告,同时,我也既不认为它是一次成熟的方法论探索,更不认为它是一个关于"讲述中国课堂故事"的完美示范。事实上,细心的读者会发现,相对来说,我对于这些片段本身所做的话语分析更加充分,而对于这些分析的讨论则是捉襟见肘。这是因为,虽然这些片段已经看过成百上千遍,我依然不觉得自己完全悟到了其中的奥妙,我对它们的理解依然是"摇摇晃晃"的,只能算是一些暂时性的想法。

我希望读者将本文视为一封邀请函。通过本文,我期待读者看到,即使在课时紧张、班额大、考试压力大的中国课堂上,我们的教师也能够创造出精妙而富有教学智慧的"回音",促进学生的课堂参与和学习。这些"回音"(以及其他的话语实践)和已有文献所讨论的形态有细微的差别,而这样的细微所引向的,是中国教育文化与实践的无限广大。最后,回到篇首的问题,我的想法是,这些细微的差别就是"枝蔓丛生",而观察、描述和分析这些差别,从而向中国教育的无限广大敞开,就是值得课堂研究者尽最大努力去做的。

参考文献

[1] 肖思汉.如何呈现一场课堂互动[J].全球教育展望,2020(12):13-26.

[2] Sandoval, W. A., Enyedy, N., Redman, E. H., & Xiao, S. Organising a Culture of Argumentation in Elementary Science [J]. International Journal of Science Education, 2019(13): 1848-1869.

[3] O'Connor, M. C. & Michaels, S. Aligning Academic Task and Participation Status through Revoicing: Analysis of a Classroom Discourse Strategy [J]. Anthropology & Education Quarterly, 1993(4):318-335.

[4] O'Connor, M. C. & Michaels, S. Shifting Participant Frameworks: Orchestrating Thinking Practices in Group Discussion [A]. Hicks, D. (Ed.), Discourse, Learning, and Schooling [C]. Cambridge University Press, 1996:63-103.

[5] McNeil, L. Using Talk to Scaffold Referential Questions for English Language Learners [J]. Teaching and Teacher Education, 2012(3):396-404.

[6] Bae, H., Glazewski, K., Brush, T., & Kwon, K. Fostering Transfer of Responsibility in the Middle School PBL Classroom: An Investigation of Soft Scaffolding [J]. Instructional Science, 2021(7):337-363.

[7] Enyedy, N., Rubel, L., Castellón, V., Mukhopadhyay, S., Esmonde, I., & Secada, W.

Revoicing in a Multilingual Classroom [J]. Mathematical Thinking and Learning, 2008(2):134 - 162.

[8] Flood, V. J. Multimodal Revoicing as an Interactional Mechanism for Connecting Scientific and Everyday Concepts [J]. Human Development, 2018(3):145 - 173.

[9] Alibali, M. W., Nathan, M. J., Boncoddo, R., & Pier, E. Managing Common Ground in the Classroom: Teachers Use Gestures to Support Students' Contributions to Classroom Discourse [J]. ZDM, 2019(2):347 - 360.

[10] 张娟娟,陈旭远,范会敏,毛清芸.新课改改了什么:基于课堂话语变革的探索——以J省D小学30年课堂教学视频分析为例[J].全球教育展望,2022(3):78 - 93.

[11] 张光陆,李娜.课堂争论对学生深度学习的影响:基于交互论证分析[J].宁波大学学报(教育科学版),2022(2):21 - 29.

[12] 宋歌.理解科学学习过程中的话语认同——基于课堂论证的互动分析[J].当代教育论坛,2019(3):112 - 120.

[13] 郁志珍.小学科学教师回音(Revoicing)话语策略的实证研究[D].上海:华东师范大学,2019.

[14] 秦乐琦.小学数学课堂回音的话语分析[D].上海:华东师范大学,2022.

[15] 任冰尔,孙丽丽.课堂互动中的教师回音话语:类型、结构与功能——以小学数学课堂的"回音"话语为例[J].上海教师,2022(6):81 - 94.

[16] Sum, E. S. W. & Kwon, O. N. Classroom Talk and the Legacy of Confucian Culture in Mathematics Classroom [J]. Teaching and Teacher Education, 2020(2):102964.

[17] Hyland, K. Talking to the Academy: Forms of Hedging in Science Research Articles [J]. Written Communication, 1996(2):251 - 281.

[18] Gumperz, J. J. Contextualization and Understanding [A]. Duranti, A. & Goodwin, C. (Eds.), Rethinking Context: Language as an Interactive Phenomenon [C]. Cambridge: Cambridge University Press, 1992:229 - 252.

[19] [苏联]巴赫金.巴赫金全集(第三卷)[M].石家庄:河北教育出版社,2009:71.

[20] [苏联]巴赫金.巴赫金全集(第四卷)[M].石家庄:河北教育出版社,2009:60.

[21] Ho, I. T. Are Chinese Teachers Authoritarian? [A]. Watkins, D. & Biggs, J. B. (Eds.), Teaching the Chinese Learner: Psychological and Pedagogical Perspectives [C]. Comparative Education Research Centre, Hong Kong University, 2001:99 - 114.

[22] Chen, X. Meaning-making of Chinese Teachers in the Curriculum Reform [A]. Zhang, H. & Pinar, W. F. (Eds.), Autobiography and Teacher Development in China: Subjectivity and Culture in Curriculum Reform [C]. London and New York: Palgrave Macmillan, 2015:193 - 211.

[23] Erickson, F. Inclusion into What?: Thoughts on the Construction of Learning, Identity, and

Affiliation in the General Education Classroom [A]. Speece, D. & Keogh, B.K. (Eds.), Research on Classroom Ecologies: Implications for Inclusion of Children with Learning Disabilities [C]. Mahwah, NJ: Lawrence Erlbaum, 1996.

[24] McDermott, R. Social Relations as Contexts for Learning in School [J]. Harvard Educational Review, 197747(2):198-213.

[25] 肖思汉,刘畅. 课堂话语如何影响学习——基于美国课堂话语实证研究的述评[J]. 教育发展研究,2016(24):45-54.

[26] 罗素丽. 爱的回音[J]. 广东教育,2016(9):33-34.

[27] 芦阳. 音乐欣赏:撞响学生心中的回音壁[J]. 学苑教育,2014(23):78.

[28] 贾宪章."回音":不可省略的旋律[J]. 教书育人,2011(2):7.

Interdisciplinarity for Enhanced Teaching and Learning of Science: Perspectives from School-Based Projects in the United Kingdom

Professor Sibel Erduran

University of Oxford

United Kingdom

Abstract

The rapid changes in science and society during the last decade have demonstrated the need for readiness to address the uncertain future. This need has been conceptualized as "future-oriented skills", which are a set of skills that students should be able to acquire through formal and informal educational settings in order to address future challenges. Current as well as future challenges involve a wide range of misinformation being propagated about issues related to science and socio-scientific issues. For example, there are individuals who claim that the earth is flat, and that climate change is a hoax. Contemporary educational landscape is thus in a position to put more emphasis on secondary students' acquisition of skills where the credibility of claims is evaluated relative to evidence and rigorous justification. Future-oriented skills such as critical thinking skills are increasingly important for regular citizens to function in society including how people deal with major health emergencies like the Covid – 19 pandemic. Argumentation, or the justification of knowledge claims with evidence and reasons, is one aspect of critical thinking skills and it has emerged as a significant educational goal, advocated in international curricula, and investigated through school-based research. In this presentation, I will review school-based funded research projects focusing on interdisciplinary investigations conducted as part of OARS, FEDORA and SciKids projects carried out in the United Kingdom in collaboration with international partners. All projects have collected and analyzed data through qualitative and quantitative methodologies to illustrate how interdisciplinary investigations can enhance the quality of education particularly with respect to future-oriented skills including argumentation. Findings from these projects will be shared.

Keywords: argumentation; scientific literacy; nature of science; future-oriented science education; 21st Century Skills

The talk today will address research focusing on Interdisciplinarity for Enhanced Teaching and Learning of Science and I will be presenting some perspectives from school-based projects from the United Kingdom. These projects have been funded by different funding agencies. For the OARS project, I would like to acknowledge Templeton World Charity Foundation. FEDORA project has been funded by the European Union Horizon 2020 Program. And the SciKids project has been funded by the United Arab Emirates University.

If we question the nature of education nowadays in comparison to what education has been and schooling has been for many years, we can reflect on the nature of education and to what extent we might have actually made progress in terms of how science is taught and learned in schools. Often, we see similar patterns of behavior and interactions and content in schools around the world. We can question the extent to which educational innovation is actually making an impact at the level of schools nowadays in comparison to what we have been doing traditionally. For example, are we teaching students in the same way, in terms of one teacher in front of the classroom, carrying out a conversation? Or are we changing the dynamics of interactions in the classroom? We can question the extent to which the curricula might have changed across the years.

But the reason why I'm raising this issue of innovation is that in science education we have a legacy of an emphasis on *what* we know rather than *how* we know and *why* we know. This typically is followed with a recipe following approach, where the students replicate known experiments and investigations, as opposed to authentic scientific practices, where they investigate unknown problems on their own to generate knowledge. Another legacy in science education is that we have discrete school subjects like chemistry, biology, and physics, as opposed to interdisciplinary approaches, such as STEM approaches, that might attempt to solve complex issues and problems. And you will notice that I have a picture of some children from some years ago, an old picture of classroom situations. I think this is intentional, because I want to emphasize that some of these legacies of science education that still continue to this day are probably impediments to innovation in science education.

Why is that a problem? The outcome of the way that we've been doing schooling is, that we know from research, that many people leave school without basic knowledge or appreciation of science. We're not motivating them sufficiently. Their motivation decreases in time. They don't make choices about science careers, and their choices decline in time, particularly when subjects get streamlined into the specific domains, such as physics, biology, and chemistry in high schools.

So, why is this a problem at all, anyway? Well, we live in an age of misinformation. With the advent of the Internet, there's a lot of information out there, where they touch on scientific knowledge and scientific literacy, where students are placed in a position to judge and evaluate information and there is a lot of propagation of misconceptions about scientific knowledge. Some of these issues, for example, proponents of the Flat Earth Society are claiming that our observation of the earth being a sphere is a hoax. They tend to breed mistrust in science and also demonstrate a lack of understanding about how science works. So, there's a lot of fake news, inaccurate information and students need to be able to engage with this information in their everyday lives. And also, as future citizens in society, we need to be equipping them with the skills to deal with misinformation.

Another contemporary development, obviously, which I don't need to remind you of, is that we've had the Covid – 19 pandemic, and the pandemic has shown us that it's not just enough to know particular information. We also need to be able to decide which knowledge claims are supported by evidence and reasons and *why*. For example, in the context of the Covid – 19 vaccines, we may question which vaccine has a higher efficacy and why. The scientists themselves have been engaged in these questions and we're also seeing that scientists are using a diversity of scientific methods. Sometimes they collect data about how the virus is affecting a patient's breathing. This is the kind of method where you're relying on observations and you're not manipulating any variables. For example, you're not increasing the amount of the virus in the body, you're simply seeing and observing what's happening to the patient. Another approach of a scientific method is where you conduct an experiment, you produce a hypothesis and conduct an experiment, and you test a vaccine, one vaccine or another through experimental and control groups. In this case, there is experimentation and manipulation of variables. So, there is the diversity of scientific methods, and also how we justify our scientific knowledge claims with evidence and reasons. This is authentic scientific practices and to what extent are we representing such authentic scientific practices in school science is what I'm raising as a question.

Furthermore, we're seeing increasingly that interdisciplinary problem-solving is important. This is a case from Germany. In Germany, apparently, one of the German states, apart from scientists and public health professionals, there were other professionals who have been engaged in trying to solve the Covid – 19 crisis. They've had philosophers, historians, theologians, jurists and they've all advised the State about how to go about solving the problem. So, we're seeing that there is a need for interdisciplinary problem-solving and interdisciplinary collaboration. This is an authentic practice in the context of the pandemic that has implications for education. It gets us to question about how we are representing such authentic practices in society in schooling to prepare the students for their future.

Some of the skills that I'm highlighting here are often called the "21st Century Skills", and there are skills such as critical thinking and problem-solving. They're required in society and workplaces. And this is part of a growing international movement, focusing on skills to master preparation for success in rapidly changing, digital societies and knowledge economies. And there is the need for interdisciplinary engagement and cross-subject consultations.

With that background, I would like to now focus on some school-based research projects that we have been carrying out in order to highlight how we have been addressing these problems. All of these projects have used different methodologies and I know this forum is focusing on methodological approaches as well. In our work reviews, we adopt mixed-methods approaches where we've used quantitative and qualitative research methods. And the works that I'll be presenting have been published widely. I'll direct you to some of our websites where you can read further on these projects.

The first project that I will talk about is the "OARS project", the Oxford Argumentation in Religion and Science Project. All of these projects have various components and they are far more extensive than I can present today. I will focus on particular aspects of each project, but they are actually a lot more inclusive and broader in scope. And I'm happy to talk about each of them later if you have any questions. In the case of the OARS project, I will focus on the teachers' engagement in interdisciplinary context. This is important because ultimately, if we want the students to have engagement in interdisciplinary context, we need to get the teachers trained to be able to do the same with their students. Because traditionally, they're not educated themselves in interdisciplinary context.

The second project is the "FEDORA Project", which is about Future-Oriented Science Education. Here I will focus on a different stakeholder, policy makers' recommendations for what we should be focusing on in science education, and in the science curriculum. This will also point to the quantitative surveys in a different methodology, the Delphi methodology that we've been using in addressing the questions around policy makers' views.

The third project is the "SciKids Project" where we've situated science in context in early years teachers' engagement about nature of science. This is a particular project where we've engaged with teacher's professional development. I'll show some strategies that we've used to engage teachers, especially early years teachers, preschool level teachers who might have limited backgrounds in science.

I'll start with the OARS project. The project has a website: OARSeducation.com. We have video clips and resources and our publications are all listed on this website, if you would like to have a look at it. In the context of the OARS project, we brought together science and religious education teachers in England. There were 30 teachers from 15 schools and we've done workshops with them. The point here was to engage them in meaningful discussions about how arguments are built in science and religious education. We capitalized on teachers-distributed expertise and we wanted them to learn from each other through this goal of promoting argumentation. When I say 'argumentation', I mean evidence-based reasoning, justifying claims with evidence and reasons. We wanted to see if they can find meaningful ways and feasible ways of working together. This is particularly important in subjects that are traditionally conceived to be in opposition to each other, such as science and religious education.

What we ended up observing is that the pedagogy of argumentation differed between the religious education and the science teachers. To our surprise, the religious education teachers indicated that they use significantly more group discussions and debates in their lessons as compared to the science teachers. This is quite important in terms of promoting argumentation. If the students are not engaged in group discussions and debates, it's questionable to what extent they're involved in argumentation. So, in the context of the professional development workshops that we've done with the science and the RE teachers, there was an opportunity for the science teachers to learn about these pedagogical strategies from the other discipline and the other subject teachers.

In terms of their views of argumentation, there were differences that were quite remarkable in terms of how science and RE teachers approach what they think about argumentation. For example, evidence is construed in a different way in science versus RE. But to the extent to which they both teach, both cohorts of teachers agreed that argumentation is important, was quite uniform. So, they could find a common ground in terms of learning to teach argumentation in their lessons.

I'll now move on to the FEDORA project. This is a project that's been funded by the Horizon 2020 Program of the European Union. It's a project that is led by University of Bologna in Italy with partners from UK ourselves in as well as Lithuania, Finland and the Netherlands. The overarching goal of the project is to produce a new future-oriented approach to science education. In our case, our component of the work is to foster policy making to align science education and educational practices with some of these 21st Century Skills that I've talked about. I have links here to the project website. And also, there is an introductory video that you can watch on YouTube on the FEDORA project.

In this project, we have conducted what's called a Delphi study. We approach policy making stakeholders, people who are influential in developing curricula, assessment, professional development, and so on. we wanted to get their ideas about what are some of the pressing skills that students need to know in order to be able to deal with the challenges of the future. So, we've used the Delphi study methodology, which is about reaching consensus.

We went to the policy makers, about 35 policy makers. We sent them an online survey and we collected their responses. And we tried to reach some consensus around some of the issues that they were building up. There was agreement about certain themes and other themes were mentioned only by a few of them. So, we've collected the consensus statements and redistributed these statements back to them again, in an effort to build a consensus to derive those recommendations that will be important and is agreed by all of them across these different national contexts in Europe. The Delphi methodology has promoted this consensus building through an online questionnaire. Eventually, we will be having a national event and an international event as well, where we'll share the outcomes of this study.

Just to show you some of the data that have come out of our investigations. The policy makers viewed problem-solving, project-based learning and interdisciplinarity as well as collaboration as important future-oriented competences. Interdisciplinarity in the way that we've also worked in the OARS project where we brought together science and religious education teachers was important from the policy makers' point of view. We have produced some outputs in this project already which you can access through the website. For example, we have outlined the policymakers' views. More broadly, I've only shown you one piece of data here, we've also written some papers for practitioners, for teachers, and also a policy brief that you can access on our website.

The third project, "SciKids Project" is about early years teaching and learning, about the nature of science. Nature of science is really about understanding how science works. At early grades, you might think that this might be a bit of a tough topic for students as well as teachers and rightly so, because this is a time when students are just beginning to question some scientific problems. So we wanted to see to what extent we can support teachers in teaching nature of science.

One of the things we've done early on in our project was to administer a survey to figure out what sort of perceptions and views teachers hold about nature of science. To do that, we've used a questionnaire that we had previously designed in another context, and we have adopted this questionnaire for language. We've tried and piloted it in the United Arab Emirates to see the extent to which there might be reliable conclusions to be drawn from the adaptation of this survey. We have a paper coming out soon about the adaptation of the survey in the *Journal of Science and Technological Education*. One of the findings was that teachers hold mixed perceptions about some key concepts, and roles and biases about scientific facts, as well as scientific practices, and how politics of science and models of scientific knowledge are discussed in the nature of science discussions. There were particular misconceptions about nature of science, for example, distinction of laws and theories, and so on and so forth. But the point that I wanted to emphasize here is that methodologically, we've adapted a questionnaire that was taken from another national context in Turkey to United Arab Emirates and we've adopted the language from Turkish to Arabic in order to carry out this investigation.

In terms of what we've done with the teachers themselves, we were very mindful of bringing broad, big ideas about the nature of science down to the level of early years students and teachers. So, we've taken everyday examples like baking a cake and putting in baking powder in a cake. And you have, in this case, two cartoon characters who are debating and discussing and arguing at this level of education about why a cake might rise with baking powder or not. This was an example that was accessible to the teachers as a professional development activity. And It's an activity where the teachers are discussing alternative claims about a particular phenomenon, and providing evidence and reasons for why the cake may rise or not. This was an activity that was appropriate to the age level of the kids and the teachers were receptive to this sort of an approach.

Other tools that we've included were tools like questioning as a meta-cognitive approach. We're getting the students and the teachers to think about the methods that they're using. For example, am I testing a hypothesis? Did I change a variable? What are the different types of methods that I might be employing in my investigation. This is a tool that we've used with teachers and they've adopted it for their own use in their teaching themselves.

In conclusion, what I've tried to do in this presentation is to show how we have approached 21st Century Skills and particularly interdisciplinarity in science education, in the context of argumentation and future-oriented skills across different levels of schooling. In the case of the OARS project, we worked with lower secondary schools. In the case of SciKids project, we've worked with early years teachers. And in both cases, we've promoted the teaching and learning of nature of science, the nature of arguments and scientific methods in science. And these are ways of reasoning and thinking in science that are often, again, under-emphasized. Because traditionally, we have emphasized scientific knowledge, the what we know, rather than how and why we know. So, we've had a focus on skills and competences. And we've also engaged with policy makers and different stakeholders, such as teachers and students. We've not only done research, but produced continual professional development strategies for teachers as a vehicle for pedagogical innovation and interdisciplinarity. In all of these projects, we've used surveys, interviews, broadly speaking, mixed methods using qualitative and quantitative approaches. Ultimately, our view is that reforming quality of education requires a change in emphasis in the content and approaches to doing school-based research and in our investigations.

Related publications

Erduran, S., Guilfoyle, L. & Park, W. (2022). Science and religious education teachers' views of argumentation and its teaching. *Research in Science Education,* 52, 655 – 673. https://doi.org/10.1007/s11165-020-09966-2.

Ioannidou, O., & Erduran, S. (2022). Policymakers' views of future-oriented skills in science education. *Frontiers in Education,* Volume 7. https://doi.org/10.3389/feduc.2022.910128.

Schofield, L., Takriti, R., Rabbani, L., AlAmirah, I., Ioannidou, O., Alhosani, N., ... Erduran, S. (2023). Early years education teachers' perceptions of nature of science. *International Journal of Science Education,* 45(8), 613 – 635. https://doi.org/10.1080/09500693.2023.2168139.

技术驱动的教师发展

Group Work in Classrooms: Dialogue, Reflection and Positive Learning Outcomes

Professor Christine Howe

Faculty of Education, University of Cambridge

Abstract

The talk on which this paper is based revolved around situations where small groups of students work together on classroom relevant tasks, without direct involvement of teachers. The talk attempted to answer two questions, using data from the over 30 studies that the speaker has been involved with. Most, but not all, of the studies were conducted in the UK, but there is every reason to believe that they have relevance to China. The first question was very simple: Can group work amongst students support their learning? The answer was 'yes' so long as group dialogue involves the students articulating contrasting ideas, giving reasons for those ideas, and evaluating ideas and reasons in the interests of task solution. The second question was: Can the positive effects of group work be enhanced through other activities? Noting that to benefit from group work, students need to reflect on and consolidate their within-group experiences, studies addressing this question focused upon what happens after group tasks are completed. It shows that what happens can make a considerable difference to how much students learn.

Keywords: group work in schools; student learning; group processes; productive dialogue; beyond-group sharing

The talk will focus on situations where small groups of students work together on classroom relevant tasks, but without direct involvement of the teacher. The use of small groups of that kind is controversial in the UK, and in some parts of the world it's completely unknown. I think it's rare in China. But my research and the research that I'm going to talk about indicates that in certain conditions, small groups can play an absolutely crucial role in supporting teaching and learning, and there is every reason to believe that this would be the case in all corners of the globe.

The talk will address two questions. The first question is very simple: Can group work amongst students support their learning? And I'll answer, yes, it can do this. It can support learning so long as group dialogue fulfills certain conditions. Having demonstrated the potential of group work, I'll move on to the second question, which is: Can the positive effects of group work be enhanced through other activities? And what I'll argue, in the second half of the talk, is that post-group events, events after the group's completed, can make a considerable difference.

I've been working on the issue of group work for over 30 years now. It's certainly not the only thing I do, but it's been a major theme of my research for a very long time, and I've been directly or indirectly involved in over 30 studies on the topic. The studies cover a very wide range of topics: Mathematics, Science, Social Science, and we've also looked at general reasoning. The studies also cover a very wide age range of students. We haven't gone much below the age of eight, but we have worked with what in the UK are 'late primary school' students: 8- to 12-year-olds. We've worked with secondary school students, high school students, and we've also worked with adults both in universities and in what in the UK are called 'Further Education colleges', colleges that focus on vocational training.

The studies all have design features in common. Firstly, they're all interventions. Sometimes the interventions are delivered by researchers who typically take the groups out of class and work with them in an intensive fashion. But in other contexts, the interventions are teacher delivered and they're part of the normal cut and thrust of classroom activity. The two approaches are complementary to each other: The first allows penetrating investigation of the processes involved and the second bears on practical applicability. I'm delighted to say that, regardless of approach, the studies all come up with very consistent findings.

There's always a three-stage design to our studies. We start with a pre-test to ascertain what students know about the topic before we get started. Then there's a group task. We've had all sorts of group sizes, pairs, trios, foursomes, sometimes much bigger groups, groups of eight even. Sometimes the tasks are presented in workbooks, sometimes they're presented via computer. We almost always record the group interaction, usually on video, sometimes by taking notes. Finally, there's always a post-test to tap what students have actually learned. The post-test follows the same format as the pre-test. We always have a delayed post-test several weeks after the group task, because we're interested in sustainable learning. Sometimes we have a post-test immediately after the group task too, so that we can map change over time. However, that varies; the key point is that there's always a delayed post-test.

Here's a couple of examples from the 30 studies. The first one is, in fact, our very first study. It was published in 1990, and it involved primary school children aged 8 to 12 years working in groups of four trying to work out the factors that determine whether objects will float or sink in a tank of water. At any point during the task, one child would have responsibility for reading task instructions from a workbook; and another child would have responsibility for putting objects in a tank of water to see whether they float or sink. Therefore, this was a physical task with children working in groups of four.

By contrast, the most recent study published in 2019 used computer-simulated tasks. Here a ball was dropped from a hot-air balloon. The balloon was sometimes stationary and was sometimes moving across the screen. The task was to plot the path that the ball will follow as it falls from the balloon. We did this study with a very wide age range. We had 10-year-old children in primary schools, three-age levels in secondary school and we also had university students. And this time, unlike the first one, the students worked in pairs.

That hopefully gives you an idea of the contrast between the studies. What do we find? Well, two key findings. Firstly, group tasks of this kind could support learning, but only when the groups contained students with differing views. When all the students had the same opinion before they started, there was no progress. Students had to have differing views. Moreover, it wasn't a question of the more advanced students tutoring the less advanced, because when we had groups like that, the more advanced students also learned. It really was a question of difference, not levels of understanding. So long as they differed, they learned.

The second key finding was that difference was important because it optimized specific forms of dialogue. The importance of dialogue needs to be underlined. The key dialogue involved firstly, the students articulating their contrasting ideas, that is making alternative proposals about task solution. Secondly, it involved giving reasons for these ideas. Thirdly, it involved evaluating both the proposals and the reasons in the interests of task solution. We found that pattern in absolutely every single study where we looked at dialogue, regardless of topic, group size, mode of presentation, student age or whatever, it was a very consistent finding.

Here are two examples of what I would regard as productive dialogue given what I've just said. The first one is with very young children. They were nine years of age, talking about floating and sinking. It comes from that very first study. Note how they're talking. Gemma starts by talking about size; Carolanne talks about weight. Yvonne brings in shape. They also talk about the material that the thing is made of, that it's a rubber ring. So, a lot of reasons are being put forward for the ideas, for the children's thinking about whether these objects will float or sink.

Gemma: Both float because they're the same size.

Carolanne: No, but that's heavier, that's heavier than the block.

Gemma: But just a wee bit so it'll float.

Yvonne: What about the shape?

Gemma: It wouldnae float.

Yvonne: Rubber ring. Float. Float.

Dorothy: No sink, cos of the curved shape.

And here's an episode from 17-year-olds from that recent study. Jenny seems to believe that when a ball's dropped from a moving balloon, it will start by going straight down but then as it gets near the ground, it'll move. It'll divert a bit like the J-shape of an umbrella handle upside down, whereas Angela thinks it'll just fall straight down. They're articulating their contrasting ideas and giving reasons. Again, a highly productive dialogue. Jenny and Angela make massive progress from pre- to post-test.

Jenny: Right next. Okay it's the heavy one, right? Yeah. The balloon moves. It goes that way, so I'd say it ... Well it goes that way.

Angela: But it's heavy, it's the heavy one.

Jenny: Yeah, so it goes straight and then in the end it would drift, you know? Like I'd say the first goes straight, the second as well, and then it goes a bit like that.

Angela: Yeah, probably.

Jenny: Well, it's moving in that direction, so it goes like that doesn't it?

Angela: Well, it also goes straight down because it's the heavy one.

Jenny: I'd say there's a slight move in the end because you know it's moving. It should be left, shouldn't it?

So, what did we learn in general from those studies? Firstly, group work can be effective. Secondly, the conditions within which it is effective include promoting a specific form of dialogue. So, the message here is that teachers should not only use small groups in classrooms but also try to promote the key forms of dialogue. But is promoting the dialogue sufficient to maximize progress? That's a question I've also been asking, and the reason I've been asking it is because of what we found about the processes by which group work has its effects.

Actually, you may be a little surprised to hear this, but we found that progress does not depend on good group task performance. Some of our groups worked out a good solution to the task they were working on, but other groups came up with solutions that were no better than where the students were at pretest and were sometimes even worse than where they were at pretest. And it didn't matter at all: so long as they experienced the key form of dialogue, and held contrasting differing opinions, then they progressed. It didn't matter at all what the group task solution was like.

Progress, on the other hand, did depend on students thinking very carefully after the group about the ideas that they'd heard, coordinating these ideas, reflecting on them, evaluating them, and bringing them all together. This is a post-group event. They have to think about the group task after it's completed. In several studies I've explored what we might do in the post-group period to support this process of reflection and learning.

For example, in a very recent study published in 2020, I explored the implications of what I call beyond-group sharing, specifically situations where students explain what happened in their group session to students who didn't participate in it. I had long suspected that the benefits of group work would be boosted if students did this, my argument being that in providing these explanations, they're having to reflect on and bring together what happened in their own group.

My study of sharing had a big sample of 71 classrooms with students all aged 10 to 11 years, it included lots of sessions of group work in each of these classrooms, and it used rating scales to assess the quality of the group dialogue. I found sharing after roughly a quarter of group work sessions, but there was a lot of variation across the classroom: Some classrooms never got the students to engage in sharing, but in others 86% of the group work was followed up with sharing.

It is important to highlight two types of sharing. The first type involved students joining new small groups, and reporting on what their previous group had been doing. One example of this that I observed occurred when the students were working on the solar system. The second type was where the teacher had divided the class into lots of small groups: They all worked on the same topic in their groups and then the teacher brought the whole class together to hold a plenary session where each group in turn would tell the whole class what had taken place. I don't think there's any need to differentiate these two types of sharing; they should both be effective from the point of view of getting students to reflect on their group work.

The results of this recent study are very encouraging. Firstly, they show once more that the quality of group work matters when quality was defined in terms of the dialogue that I was talking about earlier. If the dialogue was of high quality within the group, then there was a strong, positive association with measures of student learning-and this time the measures included both a reasoning test and absolutely critical national tests in literacy and mathematics, tests that the government requires virtually all primary school students to take at the end of the year. In addition, crucial to what I'm highlighting just now, beyond-group sharing had added value. It too predicted scores on those national tests and on the reasoning test, and it also predicted scores on a science test. Therefore, beyond-group sharing helps the students reflect on what happened in their group work and this is productive.

While beyond-group sharing takes place immediately after groups, I've also been interested in longer-term post-group support. I'd like to mention very briefly a study I did about 20 years ago. Again, working with the topic of floating and sinking, where, as well as giving the students group tasks, much like what I described above, I also exposed the students to relevant demonstrations. Two, four and six weeks after the group tasks, these demonstrations indicated the role of object mass in determining whether objects would float or sink, the role of object size, the role of object density and so on. These were wordless demonstrations. Students just individually saw what happened and they didn't discuss them in groups. Our finding was that the students who had previously worked in groups and then saw the demonstrations showed double the pre- to post-test gain of students who worked in groups but didn't have the demonstrations, and students who had the demonstrations but didn't work in groups. Perhaps most critically, what we also found was that the group dialogue played an absolutely critical role in priming the students to pay attention to those post group events — the events they saw in the demonstrations.

To draw some conclusions, I would like to argue that firstly, group work among students can support learning, but its effectiveness depends absolutely critically upon the form of group dialogue. Just to emphasize one more time, to be productive dialogue must include contrasting proposals, supporting these proposals with reasoning and evaluation of the proposals and reasons in the interest of solving the task. Of course, it implies that teachers should look for challenging tasks where contrast is likely. In addition, post-group events can enhance the impact of group dialogue, both events that take place immediately after group work like beyond-group sharing and events that take place later like demonstrations. Hopefully more work will be conducted to build on these results, and also to incorporate group work in the Chinese context as well as the UK.

Related publications

Howe, C. J., Rodgers, C., & Tolmie, A. (1990). Physics in the primary school: Peer interaction and the understanding of floating and sinking. *European Journal of Psychology of Education, V*, 459 – 475.

Howe, C., McWilliam, D., & Cross, G. (2005). Chance favours only the prepared mind: Incubation and the delayed effects of peer collaboration. *British Journal of Psychology, 96*, 67 – 93.

Howe, C., Tolmie, A., Thurston, A., Topping, K., Christie, D., Livingston, K., Jessiman, E., & Donaldson, C. (2007). Group work in elementary science: Organizational principles for classroom teaching. *Learning and Instruction, 17*, 549 – 563.

Howe, C., & Mercer, N. (2007). *Children's social development, peer interaction and classroom learning*. The Primary Review (Research Survey 2/1b). Cambridge: University of Cambridge.

Howe, C. (2009). Collaborative group work in middle childhood: Joint construction, unresolved contradiction, and the growth of knowledge. *Human Development, 52*, 215 – 239.

Howe, C., & Zachariou, A. (2019). Small-group collaboration and individual knowledge acquisition: The processes of growth during adolescence and early adulthood. *Learning and Instruction, 60*, 263 – 274.

Howe, C. (2020). Strategies for supporting the transition from small-group activity to student learning: A possible role for beyond-group sharing. *Learning, Culture and Social Interaction, 28*, 100471.

可视化分析支持的教师专业发展：以课堂视频数据为例

陈高伟

【摘要】 课堂教学视频被广泛应用于教师专业发展，老师可以通过观看和反思课堂视频提升课堂教学的成效。但是，视频中包含大量信息，这常常会影响老师对于视频中的关键环节的聚焦和反思。为了解决这一问题，本研究提出了一种基于可视化分析支持的视频观看方式，以促进老师对于课堂对话片段的反思、理解和讨论。报告介绍了相关实证研究，并探讨可视化分析应用于教师课堂教学专业发展的启发以及下一步的研究方向。

【关键词】 教师专业发展；课堂对话；可视化分析

【作者简介】 陈高伟/香港大学教育学院副教授

教师专业发展对于教师理解和改进课堂教学至关重要。以卡内基梅隆大学肯·科丁格（Ken Koedinger）教授团队的一项研究为例，[1] 如图 1 所示：对于学生而言，三种类型的数学问题，故事题（Story problem）、应用题（Word problem）和方程题（Equation），哪一种较难？研究结果显示，数学老师普遍认为故事题或者应用题对于学生是较难的。然而，根据学生答题的结

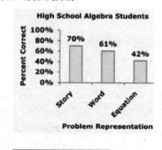

图 1　三种类型数学题

果发现,学生对于方程题的正确率最低,仅为42%。这表明,老师所想和学生实际情况存在较大偏差,科丁格称之为专家盲点(Expert blind spot)。这也意味着,作为老师,需要注重在教学中不断地了解学生、反思教学和更新认知,从而给学生提供更精确和富成效的教学支持,而教师专业发展是实现这一目标的重要途径。

一、教学视频的优势和挑战

老师在教学实践中的反思和改进有多种方法,比如专家观课、培训工作坊等。近年来,一种较为常用的方式是使用教学视频来支持老师的教学反思和专业发展。教学视频作为一种教学数据,它对于教师专业发展的作用可以从数据科学的"数据—知识—行动"的范式理解:[2]老师从课堂教学视频数据中获取信息、然后提炼为知识和理解,再将之转化为行动和决策,应用在课堂教学中。

教学视频应用于教师专业发展有很多的优势,随着技术的进步,视频录制越来越方便,视频记录可以捕捉课堂教学中的诸多细节,并可以提供多视角查看课堂教学。然而,教学视频也有很多挑战。首先,选取、编辑以及观看视频通常都较为耗时费力。其次,课堂视频中包含海量的声音、图像及动态信息,教师观看时难以聚焦。再次,面对多次录课的视频以及多个课堂的视频,教师难以做纵向和横向的比较、分析和理解。

二、教学视频分析和可视化

为了提升课堂教学视频在教师专业发展中的使用成效,本研究提出一种以可视化和学习分析增强视频数据效力的方案。举例来说,我们可以把视频里的一些特定的信息提取出来,如图2上方所示,在这一节课中,学生在三次发言中提到了其他学生的姓名,这意味着学生可能在和其他学生一起共同思考、引用其他学生观点或者对其他学生的观点进行评价等。如图2

以可视化和学习分析增强视频数据效力

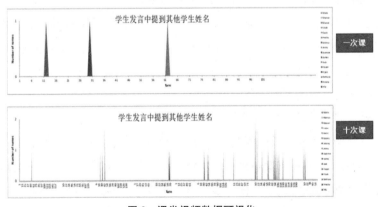

图2 课堂视频数据可视化

下方所示,我们可以把10次课的可视化一起表达出来,可以看到,随着教学的推进,学生越来越多地在课堂上提到其他学生的姓名。通过将教学视频进行可视化分析和表达,可以大大提升教学视频在教师专业发展中的使用效能。

三、以可视化分析促进教师课堂对话技巧

我们所开展的教师专业发展实证研究旨在提升教师课堂对话技巧。大致来说,老师在课堂上可以从两个维度提升师生对话。如图3所示,一个维度是通过对话促进学生个人的思考,比如老师引导学生进行补充或解释;另一个维度是以对话促进学生的共同思考,比如老师引导学生补充他人或引导学生对彼此观点的评价等。[3][4][5]

图3　促进学生课堂发言和思考

研究对象包含来自15个学校的46位初一、初二年级的数学老师,平均年龄32.7岁,平均教龄10年。教师被分成两组,实验组24位老师,对照组22位老师。参与学生人数共计1500人左右。研究方案采用了一种循环式的教师专业发展干预手段:首先,老师进行正常课堂教学和录像,然后研究小组对教师所录制课堂视频进行数据处理,形成可视化和分析结果,然后邀请实验组老师进行定期的研讨;对照组老师也会参加单独的定期研讨,但是没有可视化和学习分析支持。这种循环式干预在一学年的时间内进行了五次,平均每一到两个月一次。

在每次大约两小时的定期研讨中,实验组老师会反思自己的课堂对话以及与其他老师一起进行课堂对话的比较和讨论。通过可视化分析呈现(如图4),老师可以较为直观地看到彼此的课堂教学情况,同时,老师可以通过点击、筛选和放大可视化界面等功能,查看课堂对话细节,进行深入反思和讨论。在研讨活动结束阶段,老师会制定下一步教学改进计划。通常,不同的老师会有不同的教学改进计划,比如有些老师可能想引导更多的学生独立思考,有的老师则可能想促进学生之间有更多的共同思考等。

研究通过收集问卷、录像和访谈等数据测量实验干预效果。其中一项数据是关于老师课堂对话的信念以及课堂对话的效能的改变情况,课堂对话信念是关于老师是否相信课堂对话功能,或者是否懂得课堂对话重要,对学生学习有帮助;课堂对话效能是关于老师是否觉得自己能够引导好课堂对话,或者是否相信自己有引导和组织有效课堂对话的能力。实验结果表明,通过使用可视化分析审视课堂对话,实验组教师相对对照组教师在对话信念和对话效能

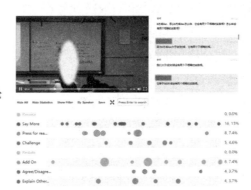

图 4　课堂对话可视化分析界面

上都有显著的提升。

另外一项对比是关于老师课堂话语类型,实验结果表明,在老师八种类型的课堂话语中有五种得到了显著提升。在师生课堂话语数量方面,结果显示实验组学生相对于对照组学生平均每次发言的字数得到显著提升。如图 5 所示,实验前,实验组学生大概每次发言是 8—9 个字,在实验后实验组提升到了 12 个字左右,这意味着学生在课堂讨论中有更充足的发言时间,每次发言可以说出更多的内容。最后,我们还做了有关学生数学学业成绩的测试,相对于对照组,实验组学生在干预后有显著的数学成绩提升。

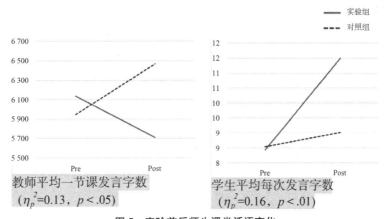

图 5　实验前后师生课堂话语变化

四、可视化分析如何促进教师反思和专业发展

总的来说,本研究通过将课堂视频进行可视化分析和呈现,有效地促进了教师对于课堂对话的反思与改进,并提升了学生课堂参与以及学业成绩。这一教师专业发展方式的启示包

含以下几个方面:首先,可视化分析可以将有意义的课堂对话提取和显示,使得老师对于课堂教学的反思更加聚焦和有效。其次,可视化分析为老师与同伴在教研上的比较与讨论提供具体的数据支持,这样老师之间的讨论也更有依据。再次,老师通过查看过往课堂教学的可视化分析报告,可以更为直观地看到自己教学的变化趋势,对于课堂教学的追踪和改进更为方便,这也有助于老师积累信心和经验,保持对教学的持续的反思和改进。为了更好地理解和促进课堂教学,将来的课堂视频可视化分析可以更为全面地呈现课堂中的信念、态度、动机和情绪等情感因素。同时,可视化分析可以通过融入人工智能等技术,为老师创造更为便利的协作式的专业发展空间,促进老师的共同进步和专业发展。

参考文献

[1] Koedinger, K.. Stanford seminar-Using big data to discover tacit knowledge and improve learning [J]. Retrieved from: https://www.youtube.com/watch?v=dNCqJP0URE8, 2014.

[2] Lazer, D., Pentland, A., Adamic, L., Aral, S., Barabási, A. L., Brewer, D., ... & Van Alstyne, M. Computational social science. *Science*, 2009, 323(5915), 721-723.

[3] Chen, G., Chan, C.K., Chan, K.K., Clarke, S.N., & Resnick, L.B. Efficacy of video-based teacher professional development for increasing classroom discourse and student learning [J]. *Journal of the Learning Sciences*, 2020, 29(4-5), 642-680.

[4] Michaels, S., O'Connor, M.C., & Resnick, L.B.. Deliberative discourse idealized and realized: Accountable talk in the classroom and in civic life [J]. *Studies in the Philosophy of Education*, 2008, 27(4), 283-297. https://doi.org/10.1007/s11217-007-9071-1.

[5] Resnick, L.B., Michaels, S., & O'Connor, M.C.. How (well structured) talk builds the mind. In D. Preiss & R. Sternberg (Eds.) [J], *Innovations in educational psychology*, 2010 (pp.163-194). Springer.

课件分析视域下的教与学：打开课堂教学黑箱的另一种路径*
——基于 OECD "全球教学洞察"项目的课件评价方法及结果发现

徐瑾劼　申昕

【摘要】 近年来，在教育领域，视频研究在我国的发展方兴未艾。视频研究不仅采集视频，以反映教师在课程实施中的行为表现，还同时采集教科书、任务单、作业和演示 PPT 等课件，以反映教师在预期课程中所设计的学习机会。OECD 在全球范围开展的"全球教学洞察"（GIT）项目的特色之一是在统一的评价维度下独立于视频单独对课件进行评分和分析，旨在从课件的视角洞察系统层面各国及地区的教学质量，以丰富教学改进的路径。本研究旨在阐释和分析 GTI 项目所运用的课件评价方法、技术以及主要的发现，以提出改进我国本地化课件评价研究的建议，包括借助教育智能化发展大规模课件评价，促进"概化理论"（G-Theory）在课件评价质量监测和保障中的应用等。

【关键词】 OECD；全球教学洞察（GTI）项目；课件分析；评价

【作者简介】 徐瑾劼/上海师范大学国际与比较教育研究院，教育部教育大数据与教育决策实验室副教授

申昕/上海师范大学国际与比较教育研究院硕士研究生

Teaching and Learning Through Lens of Artefact Analysis: Another Approach to Opening Black Box of Class Teaching — Based on Methodology and Results from GTI Project by OECD

XU Jinjie　SHEN Xin

(Research Institute of International and Comparative Education, Shanghai Normal University; Ministry of Education Big Data and Education Policy Making Laboratory, Shanghai, 200234, China)

Abstract: In recent years, video study is flourishing in the field of education in our nation. Video study not only collects videos with aim to investigate on teachers' behavior in implemented curriculum but also captures artefacts with aim to investigate on learning

---

* 本文系 2022 年度"上海浦江人才计划"资助项目"全球人才竞争背景下国际大规模教育测评的生产、传播机制及中国方案研究"（项目编号：22PJC092）的研究成果。

opportunities designed by teacher in intended curricula. Global Teaching Insights (GTI) Project, which is organized globally by OECD, features in coding and analyzing artifact data independent of video with purpose of investigation on quality of teaching practices across countries and regions from lens of artefact only and enriching methods for teaching improvement. This study attempts to propose suggestions on how to improve our local study on artifact-based evaluation research through illustrating and analyzing methodology, techniques in appraisal of artefacts used by GTI Project as well as the initial findings. Suggestions include promotion large-scale appraisal of artefacts through use of digital technology in education, application of G-Theory in quality assurance of artifact evaluation.

Keywords: OECD; Global Teaching Insights (GTI) Project; artefact analysis; evaluation

一、引言：OECD 开展 GTI 项目课件评价的缘起

打开课堂教学的"黑箱"不仅是促进教师个体专业反思和学习的有效方式，还有助于教育政策制定者发现如何将教育改革转化为有效的教学实践。一直以来，各国教育研究者致力于尝试和探索各种方法，以揭开课堂教学的"黑箱"。问卷调查是被广泛采用的方法之一，具有调查规模大、范围广且成本低的明显优势。但其也存在一些突出问题，如作答具有一定的主观性，调研者与被调研者对同一概念较易产生理解偏差，被调研者的回答是迎合社会期望的可能性等。[1]更重要的是，问卷调查在记录和捕捉师生互动等构成"教学"复杂性的关键"要素"方面有效性不足。[2]案例研究法(case study)通过对教学进行直接而密集的观察，结合对教师、学生等多主体开展的访谈，试图克服问卷调查法的上述局限性，但其自身的不足在于人力和时间上的消耗过大，虽在部分课堂的深度研究上占有优势，却较难扩大研究规模，从而使得这类研究的相关发现尚不足以支撑系统层面教育政策的改进。

经合组织(Organization of Economic Co-operation and Development，简称 OECD)也一直在探索打开教学黑箱，发现"有效教学"(effective teaching)的路径。实际上，OECD 开展"全球教学洞察"(Global Teaching Insights，简称 GTI)项目的直接动因源于学界和教育实践者对教师教学国际调查项目(Teaching and Learning International Survey，简称 TALIS)的质疑和批评，即单凭 TALIS 无法测量教学的有效性。OECD 教育与技能司在实践中意识到了单一测评工具的局限性，因此提出了基于课堂的视频研究的设想，通过收集教师及学生的自陈式数据(问卷)、师生行为数据(视频)、教学设计的文本数据(课件)以及学习结果数据(测试成绩)等多种来源的数据，记录"有效教学"产生的过程。

随着数字技术运用的普及，在教育领域开展大规模视频研究(video-based study)为实现兼顾课堂教学的复杂性及其研究发现的推广性的目标提供了可能性。视频研究采用多源取证

的方式对课堂教学进行多维度、全景式的探究。证据(evidence)的来源不仅限于教师所教课程的课堂视频录像,还包括了解学生和教师对所教课堂、学科教学及学习感受的问卷,教师自述的教学日志(teacher log)及用于教学的课件(artifact)。纵观国际性的课堂教学视频研究项目,大量的研究发现是基于问卷和视频分析而得出的结果(如 TIMSS 1995、TIMSS 1999、MET 等),而以用于课堂教学的课件为视角,洞察和反映课堂教学质量的研究数量较少。在跨国性的视频研究中,学习者视角研究项目(Learners Perspective Study,简称 LPS)和 OECD 开展的 GTI 项目不仅采集了师生问卷、课堂视频录像,同时还采集了教师在视频教学中使用到的课件。[3]然而,参加 LPS 项目的 14 个国家及地区未能在统一的评价框架、指标和量规下对所收集的课件进行评分,使得相应的分析结果较难进行跨国比较。2016 年,OECD 正式启动和开展了 GTI 项目,该项目有中国上海、日本、英国英格兰和德国等 8 个国家及地区参加,是国际上第一个对所收集到的教学课件进行单独编码和评分的跨文化课堂视频研究,为打开课堂教学的"黑箱"提供了一种新的视野和研究路径。[4]

二、GTI 项目课件评价的指标及方法

GTI 项目中所采集的课件是指教师在录像课所教班级课堂教学中使用过的所有相关辅助性教学资源,包括教案、教科书、作业(包括课内作业单和课后作业)、形成性评价工具(例如随堂测验)以及课上公开展示的可视化工具(例如学习软件和教师使用的 PPT)等。从课件来源的构成来看,通过分析课件,能够全面洞察教师在课前的预期课程(intended curricula)、课上的实施课程(enacted curricula)及课后的评价课程(assessed curricula)整个过程中为学生所提供学习机会的质量,补充问卷和视频录像难以捕捉和反映的信息,例如书面练习和作业等。为了确保课件评分结果在不同教育体系之间的可比性,GTI 项目在采集视频、问卷和课件等原始数据之前,会组织各参与国及地区的数学专家、教育研究人员和政策制定者开发出共同认可的、统一的课件评分指标和编码工具。

(一)GTI 项目课件评价的指标体系

课件主要反映的是教师提供给学生的学习机会的质量,而质量体现在学生与学科内容之间互动的水平。尽管 GTI 项目对课件进行单独的评分和结果分析,但其评价维度在设计上仍然与视频保持一致。简言之,对课件和视频的评价均在 GTI 项目对"教学质量"的概念定义和评价框架下进行。GTI 项目在对课堂教学进行评价时,把"教学"解构为课堂管理、社会情感支持、课堂话语、学科内容质量、认知参与和评价与反馈等 6 个维度。[5]课件可反映课堂话语、学科内容质量、认知参与和基于学生理解的评价与反馈(以下简称"评价与反馈")等 4 个评价维度上的表现,但其反映的信息具有局限性,并不能完全反映教学在上述 6 个评价维度上的表现,例如无法捕捉师生互动中表现出来的社会情感能力。为此,GTI 项目聚焦课件能够反映的 4 个维度,设计了 11 项课件评价指标,以综合描述教师在教案、课堂练习、作业布置、随堂测验

及讲解演示(PPT)等书面形式的辅助性资料中关注学生数学思维、基础技能以及现实应用的能力(见表1)。

表1 GTI项目课件评价的指标体系

评价维度	评价指标
课堂话语	做出解释
学科内容质量	明确的学习目标
	满足学生多样化的需求
	数学表征间的联系
	明确的模式和概括
	与现实世界的联系
	材料的准确性
认知参与	运用和比较多种数学方法
	训练技能的机会
	运用技术促进学生理解
评价与反馈	鼓励学生自我评估

资料来源：OECD. Global Teaching Insights：A Video Study of Teaching [R]. Paris：OECD Publishing，2020.

在"课堂话语"维度上，通过"做出解释"这一课件评价指标，反映了教师在教案、课堂练习、讲解演示(PPT)、作业布置及随堂测验等书面形式的辅助性资料中，要求学生通过自己的理解描述、说明、比较、论证数学概念、程序和方法的程度。该指标反映了教师对学生数学思维深度和思维表达的重视水平。

"学科内容质量"维度包括"明确的学习目标""满足学生多样化的需求""数学表征间的联系""明确的模式和概括""与现实世界的联系"和"材料的准确性"等6个课件评价指标，关注教师在教案、课堂练习、作业布置、随堂测验及讲解演示(PPT)等书面形式的辅助性资料中为学生提供的进行数学联系、推理及应用的学习机会，以及教师教学清晰度和教学设计个性化的情况。

"认知参与"维度包括"运用和比较多种数学方法""训练技能的机会"以及"运用技术促进学生理解"等3个课件评价指标，反映了教师在教案、课堂练习、作业布置、随堂测验及讲解演示(PPT)等书面形式的辅助性资料中重视学生数学思维的灵活性、开放性，重视学生基础性技能的掌握以及信息与通信技术(Information and Communication Technology，简称 ICT) 深度融入教学的程度。

在"评价与反馈"维度上，"鼓励学生自我评估"这一课件评价指标反映了教师在教案、课堂练习、讲解演示(PPT)、作业布置及随堂测验等书面形式的辅助性资料中要求学生对当前学习情况进行反思,并报告自我自信程度,包括内容的理解、技能的掌握等。该指标体现了教师对学生元认知能力的重视水平。

(二) GTI 项目课件评价的方法

1. 评分流程的设计

GTI 项目要求每个参与国家及地区随机选取 85 名初中数学教师,每名教师需围绕"一元二次方程"单元教学主题,在同一个班级拍摄 2 节课。每名教师不仅需要提交第 1 节和第 2 节课上使用到的课件,还需要提交摄录课后 1 节课上使用到的课件。因此,每 1 名教师应提交 4 节"一元二次方程"课上使用的 4 套课件,其中 2 套为在摄录课中教师教学所用课件,教师应根据教学实际发生的情况提交课件。可见,每节课的课件构成(教案、作业单、可视化材料、随堂测验等)可能会有所不同。从 GTI 项目收集到的教师课件的数量来看,平均每名教师提交课件数量最多的前三个国家及地区分别是中国上海(15.5 件)、德国(13.8 件)和墨西哥(12.03 件),最少的后三个国家及地区分别是智利(5.63 件)、哥伦比亚(7.83 件)和日本(8.03 件)。考虑到评分的工作量,GTI 项目并未采集课件中教师给予学生的反馈(例如作业上的批注和评语)以及学生的作答。这也体现了 GTI 项目的课件分析主要聚焦在教师所设计的学习机会以及所预期、计划的学生与学科内容之间的互动上。[6]

GTI 项目组根据 11 项课件评价指标,以每套课件为单位进行评分。每套课件均由随机分配的 2 名具有资质的评分人员进行评分。每套课件在 11 个评价指标上的得分取 2 名评分人员评分结果的均值。每名教师在 11 个课件评价指标上的得分取 4 套课件评分结果的均值(如表 2 所示)。

表 2　GTI 项目课件评价指标评分结果的产生过程示例

	评分人员 1	评分人员 2	课件/套的评分结果均值
第 1 套课件	3	2	2.5
第 2 套课件	2	2	2
第 3 套课件	2	3	2.5
第 4 套课件	1	1	1
教师 1			2

2. 评分量规的设计

除"材料的准确性",其他 10 个课件评价指标的量规均为 1—3 分:"1"代表低水平,"2"代表中等水平,"3"代表高水平。其中,"2"和"3"之间的差异主要体现在学生的主体性和认知参与深度这两个方面。"主体性"(agency)指的是学生在进行数学思维过程中的主动性和自主性。以"数学表征间的联系"这一课件评价指标为例,如果课件反映的是教师把图形和方程进行了联系或者教科书中已展示了两者的联系,而非教师让学生对两者进行联系,那么该指标的得分为2,不能达到3分。"认知参与"指的是在认知技能的要求上,课件中教师提供的学习机会是否达到高阶水平。以"运用技术促进学生理解"这一课件评价指标为例,如果教师仅是把信息技术作为一种辅助教学的手段(PPT展示教学内容、播放视频等),而不是利用技术让学生去探索数学关系(函数与图像),增进他们对"函数"这一概念的理解,那么该指标的得分为2,不能达到3分。需要特别说明的是,"材料的准确性"指标的量规为1—2,其中1表示"课件中所呈现的数学内容有重大错误"(例如定义错误、条件缺失等),而"2"表示"课件中所呈现的数学内容是准确的"。

3. 评分结果的可靠性检验

通过统计评分人员评分结果的一致性来体现可靠性。GTI项目课件评价通过"完全一致"(Exact Agreement)比例和"评分组内相关系数"(Intraclass Correlation Coefficient,简称ICC)这两个指标来综合反映评分人员判断的一致性(如表3所示)。ICC指数的范围在0—1,均值越高则说明评分人员对同一套课件的判断一致性越高。

表3 GTI项目课件评分结果一致性检验

国家/地区	完全一致百分比均值	评分ICC均值
智利	84%	0.71
哥伦比亚	76%	0.51
英国英格兰	74%	0.49
德国	75%	0.60
日本	69%	0.50
西班牙马德里	81%	0.64
墨西哥	78%	0.60
中国上海	71%	0.40

资料来源:OECD. Global Teaching Insights Technical Report[R]. Paris:OECD Publishing,2020.

三、GTI项目课件分析视域下教学质量水平的比较

根据课件分析对教学质量做出可信度高的判断正在成为辅助或替代通过直接的课堂观察或基于录像课的视频分析对教师进行评价的方式之一。[7]OECD开展的GTI项目展现了上述前景,旨在通过对课件的评价在系统层面回答课件所反映的课堂教学质量的平均水平如何。

参加GTI项目的8个国家及地区在地域和文化上具有一定代表性,包括来自东亚的日本和中国上海,欧洲的英国英格兰、德国和西班牙马德里以及拉丁美洲的墨西哥、哥伦比亚和智利。因此,这8个国家及地区在11项课件评价指标上的表现能够在课件这一独特的视角下反映目前全球教学质量发展的特点。需要说明的是,由于8个国家及地区在"材料的准确性"该项指标上的评分结果无区分度,几乎都赋值为"2"。因此,GTI项目组并未把该指标纳入到国际比较和分析中。纳入分析的10项课件评价指标的得分范围在1—3分,其中"1—1.5分"表

示各项指标所描述的学习机会"几乎没有或没有"出现;设定"1.5—2.5分"或"2.5—3分"表示各项指标所描述的学习机会出现了,但学习机会的质量(学生主体性和认知参与的水平)处于中度或高度水平。根据上述标准设定,结合8个国家及地区在10项课件评价指标的得分情况(如表4所示)可以发现和归纳出共同存在的优势及挑战。

表4 GTI项目8个国家及地区在课件评分指标上的表现(均值)

课件评价指标	中国上海	日本	英国英格兰	德国	墨西哥	西班牙马德里	哥伦比亚	智利
做出解释	2.02	1.62	1.42	1.57	1.41	1.06	1.13	1.16
明确的学习目标	2.91	2.21	2.29	1.94	2.42	1.68	1.92	2.33
满足学生多样化的需求	1.22	1.16	1.52	1.19	1.05	1.37	1.01	1.04
数学表征间的联系	1.29	2.28	2.14	2.40	2.28	1.65	1.81	1.86
明确的模式和概括	1.96	1.47	1.32	1.44	1.33	1.09	1.09	1.07
与现实世界的联系	1.36	1.91	1.31	1.73	1.92	1.45	1.45	1.51
运用和比较多种数学方法	1.86	1.77	1.40	1.89	1.51	1.61	1.54	1.58
训练技能的机会	2.88	2.03	2.84	2.44	2.24	2.64	2.06	2.48
运用技术促进学生理解	1.02	1.04	1.16	1.29	1.15	1.16	1.08	1.09
鼓励学生自我评估	1.38	1.31	1.15	1.11	1.09	1.02	1.01	1.10

注:10项课件评价指标的得分范围均在1—3分。
资料来源:OECD. Global Teaching Insights Technical Report[R]. Paris: OECD Publishing, 2020.

(一)展示学习目标的机会充足

"明确的学习目标"这一课件评价指标主要反映的是教师在教案及课上演示的材料(PPT或板书)中展示的学习目标的清晰程度。评分结果显示,8个国家及地区该项指标的均值都在1.5分以上。除哥伦比亚(14.5%)、西班牙马德里(18.8%)外,在大部分国家及地区,仅5%的教师该项指标的评分结果在1—1.5分。这表明大部分参加GTI项目的数学教师都能以书面形式向学生明确表达学习目标。然而,各国及地区间教师在该项课件指标上的差异体现在"1.5—2.5分"和"2.5—3分"之间教师的比例上。该差异在课件上体现为教师对学习目标表达的具体化程度。在细节性强的学习目标中,教师会对学生的应知应会作出明确说明。从整体看,除中国上海外(94.1%),参加GTI项目的各国及地区的大部分教师在课件中所展示的学习目标的细节性程度都未达到高度水平(2.5—3分)。

(二)训练技能的机会充足

"训练技能的机会"这一课件评价指标反映的是在课堂练习及课后作业中教师要求学生对某项技能反复练习以达到熟练水平的机会。该项指标的均值在2.5—3分说明技能训练机会频繁,具体体现在课件中教师针对同一项技能或程序的训练设计了约有5道及以上的练习题。从整体看,该项课件评价指标在8个国家及地区的均值都在2.0分以上。这说明在所有参加GTI项目的国家及地区,教师提供给学生进行重复技能或程序训练的机会强度至少平均处于中度水平。其中,98.8%的中国上海教师和94.1%的英国教师该项指标的均值在2.5—3分,机会强度处于高度水平。

(三) 满足学生多样化的需求和技术深度融入教学的机会不足

21世纪课堂的典型特征之一是技术在教学中的深度融合。"深度融合"的目的是赋能教师,通过数字技术手段实现规模化教育的个性化培养,满足学生个别化学习需求。然而,GTI项目的课件评分结果发现:第一,各国及地区普遍存在教师信息技术运用深度不够。在8个国家及地区中,90%及以上的教师"运用技术促进学生理解"的均值仅在1—1.5分,德国除外(68.0%)。这表明大部分教师在数学课堂上只是出于展示、分享和交流的目的运用信息技术,例如PPT、实物投影仪等,很少利用技术促进学生计算、画图、自我评估(软件的运用)及对抽象数学概念的理解。第二,根据学生能力水平提供个别化支持的意识不足。在参加GTI项目的国家及地区中,80%及以上的教师在"满足学生多样化的需求"这一课件评价指标的得分仅在1—1.5分,英国英格兰(50.6%)和西班牙马德里(64.9%)除外。这表明大部分教师在教案、作业和学习任务设计中未能根据不同学生能力水平提供分层分类的学习机会。

(四) 培养学生元认知技能的机会不足

在GTI项目中,通过所收集的课件发现,教师提供给学生动用"元认知技能"的机会指教师在较大程度上要求学生以书面形式对自己的学习进程做出具体判断,而不是对本节课的内容进行总结或与其他同学的想法进行比较。从"鼓励学生自我评估"这一课件评价指标来看,除日本(71.9%)和中国上海(61.2%)外,其余6个国家及地区90%以上的教师都未能要求学生以书面形式对自己的学习进行反思或评价,该项指标评价得分仅在1—1.5分。值得的注意的是,36.5%的中国上海教师会以书面形式要求学生对所学内容进行笼统的评价,例如"你在多大程度上有自信和把握理解了'一元二次方程'这个概念"。

四、GTI项目课件分析视域下教学质量差异的分析

(一) 甄别影响课件质量的教师因素:概化理论(G-Theory)的运用

课件评分结果反映的是课件的质量,而课件的质量则体现了教学质量,尤其集中反映了以学习内容为载体的学习机会的质量。显然,教师个体及其授课内容、评分人员的评价及评分人员与不同教师的交叉影响(例如评分人员可能会对一些教师给出较高的评分)会直接影响课件质量。换言之,考虑到测量误差(例如评分人员对评分标准理解的偏差等),课件评分只能部分反映教师个体间存在的真正有意义的差异。而如果要发现这些"有意义的"差异,即由教师差异而导致的课件质量的差异,则有必要甄别出各种导致评分结果差异的来源(例如源于测量工具的误差、源于工具使用者的误差等)及其在总差异中的占比。为此,GTI项目采用"概

化理论"(Generalizability Theory,简称 G-Theory)的方法对课件评分结果进行差异来源的解构分析。概化理论运用方差分析技术,将测量结果的总变异分解成测量目标(即测量所要描述的特征)的变异和测量侧面(即影响和制约测量目标的各种因素和条件,包括测量工具、测量环境、测量时间等)的变异。一般而言,当测量目标引起的变异所占比重较大时,表明测量具有较高水平的信度(reliability)。该方法已被广泛应用于教师行为测量的可信度检验中。[8]与经典测量理论(Classic Test Theory)相比,概化理论的特色在于对构成差异的来源进行细分化的估计。

鉴于GTI项目中的课件评价,每名教师提交了4节课上使用到的4套课件,每套课件均由随机选取的2名具有资质的评分人员进行编码。因此,课件评分结果上的差异可以细分为5个构成的部分:(1)教师间的差异;(2)教师所教课程内容的差异(课件评分结果可能会因教师在不同节课上教授内容的不同而出现差异);(3)评分人员间的差异(例如一些评分人员总是更为严格);(4)评分人员和不同课之间交叉影响的差异(同一名评分人员评同一名教师所教不同节课的差异;(5)残余的差异(模型尚未能解释到的差异)。本研究利用线性混合随机效应模型,根据每个参加国家及地区在10项课件指标上的得分分别估算出上述5种差异来源的对应占比。其数学模型如下:

$$\rho = \frac{Var(c)}{Var(c) + \frac{Var(r)}{n_R} + \frac{Var(l:c)}{n_L} + \frac{Var(rxl:c)}{n_R n_L} + \frac{Var(error)}{n_R n_L}}$$

注:c代教师,r代表评分人员,$l:c$代表教师所教课的内容,$rxl:c$代表评分人员与不同课的交叉影响,n_R代表每套课件评分人员的数量,n_L代表每名教师提交的课件数量。

(二)教师所教课的内容是影响课件评分差异的主要因素

基于线性混合随机效应模型对各国及地区教师各项课件指标得分的方差分析结果显示,在五种差异来源中,教师所教课的内容在大部分课件评价指标得分的总差异中占比最高,即可视其为差异的首要因素。[9]从8个国家及地区GTI项目的11项课件指标评分结果的总体情况看,约38%的评分结果差异来源自教师所教课的内容不同。该项差异来源占比最高的课件评价指标是"与现实世界的联系",比例达67%。这表明在GTI项目中教师以书面形式为学生提供与现实世界联系的学习机会在其所上的4节课上的分布不均衡。在有些课上的机会很多,但在一些课上则较少甚至没有机会。而导致机会不均衡的主要原因在于课的内容发生了变化。相对而言,评分人员和教师间的差异在构成整个评分结果差异的来源中占比较小。这表明,平均而言,在GTI项目的11项课件评价指标上,不同的评分人员及不同的教师在课件得分上的一致性相对较高。

一般而言,应关注差异来源的分析结果中教师得分变化及差异较大的评价指标。在GTI

项目的 11 项课件评价指标中,"与现实世界的联系"(8 个国家及地区该项指标均值的标准差为 0.52)和"数学表征间的联系"(8 个国家及地区该项指标均值的标准差为 0.50)这两项课件评价指标得分的差异较大。如图 1 所示,根据差异构成的分析发现,教师所教课的内容是影响"与现实世界的联系"指标评分结果的主要因素。但更有意义的发现是,除日本和西班牙马德里外,其他国家及地区的教师差异达到了 10% 以上,尤其中国上海(22%)、哥伦比亚(21%)和智利(28%)达到了 20% 以上。这表明,在这些国家对教师进行干预或将有效提升学生通过课件获得更多与现实世界联系的机会。

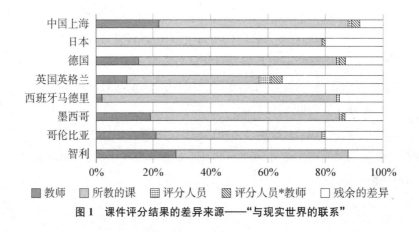

图 1　课件评分结果的差异来源——"与现实世界的联系"

如图 2 所示,"教师所教的课"仍然是"数学表征间的联系"这一指标评分差异的主要来源。但与"与现实世界的联系"这一指标比较后发现,该指标评分结果中未被解释的差异(残余的差异)比例较高。这提示教育研究人员需要进一步改进课件评价工具,以发现其他影响教师行为的因素。

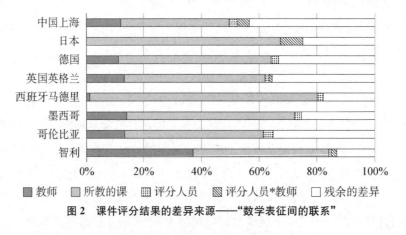

图 2　课件评分结果的差异来源——"数学表征间的联系"

但从影响上述两项课件评价指标评分结果的差异构成看,评分人员及评分人员与教师的交叉影响对评分结果的差异性影响较小。这也在一定程度上反映了 GTI 项目课件评价工具得到了严格、统一的操作和运用。

五、启示及建议

在GTI项目中,课件评价独立于视频分析单独开展,并在GTI项目课堂教学评价的统一框架下,洞察了教师以书面形式向学生提供的学习机会的质量。此种分析方法和研究路径在国际视频研究发展历程中具有里程碑意义。意义不仅限于在系统层面对各国及地区促进课堂变革提供了新思路,更有价值的是为提升课堂教学评价的科学性、规范性和有效性提供了方法和技术上的借鉴。

(一)利用教育智能化发展使课件评价成为一种常态化的教学评价方式,可作为对课堂观察或视频分析的有力补充

课件评价是否或在多大程度上能替代问卷调查、课堂观察或基于录像课的视频分析的问题,一直受到国内外学者的持续关注和探讨。已有研究表明,整体而言,基于课件对教学质量进行评价所得出的结果与通过课堂观察所得出的评价结果,两者的相关性并不高,但未出现负相关,尤其在诸如教学内容质量、评价及反馈等评价维度上两者间的相关度较强。[10][11][12]但仍然要认识到,基于所收集的课件是无法对"师生互动"(课堂话语)的质量进行细致分析和评价的。研究证实,以视频和课件分析相结合的方式对教学质量进行测评所得出的结果比单一通过视频或课件分析而得出的结果更具可信度,且相关性也更强。[13]相对于视频录像的采集和切片式的分析,课件评价的优势在于成本低,但需要教师对课件资料进行保存、存档、扫描和有序排放,可能会产生额外工作负担。但在技术赋能教师的时代背景下,教育全面的数字化转型为课件的大规模采集和评价智能化提供了可操作性。

(二)借鉴GTI项目课件评价质量保障的方法与技术,提升视频研究的科学性和规范性

GTI项目对课件评价质量保障贯穿于整个评价工作的始末:评分前的评分人员资格认证、评分过程中的质量监测以及评分后基于结果的信度检验。第一步,在评分之前需组织评分候选人对评分标准、编码工具进行集中培训,并以考核的方式进行资格确认。这有利于确保评分人员对课件评价工具有一致性的认知和理解,从而最大程度地降低主观认识或偏见的可能性。第二步,在评分过程中引入"校准"(calibration)环节,把具有"标准分"的课件周期性混入到待评的课件中,以检查评分人员的判断。第三步,对课件评分结果进行信度检验。GTI项目课件评价对11项课件评价的结果进行了相关分析和信度检验。11个评价维度的相关系数范围在接近于0至0.65之间。这表明各评价指标的关联度处于弱到中度水平,整体上看,能为洞察教学质量提供各类独特且有差别化的信息。此外,GTI项目还统计了参加国家及地区在课件评分结果上的信度,范围在0.11—0.61。上述GTI项目课件评价质量保障的流程及方法也适用于视频研究中对问卷调查和视频分析结果的信效度检验。此外,概化理论用于对评分

结果差异来源的分析有助于发现因评分质量导致的结果差异,例如评分人员对评分标准及编码理解一致性较差。若该部分差异在评分结果总差异中的占比越大,则表示评分结果并不能充分反映教学质量的差异是因教师而产生的,因而也无法根据评分结果提出有效的教学改进策略。

(三)基于 GTI 项目课件评价结果开展国家及地区的个案研究,根据评价指标有针对性地甄选和汇集"高质量"课件范例

对参加国家及地区在 GTI 项目中 11 项课件评分结果的均值的离散程度进行比较后发现,尽管在诸多指标上各国及地区的均值水平相近,但国家及地区内部的教师间差异更大。以"训练技能的机会"这一课件评价指标为例,8 个国家及地区的得分均值水平都较高,处于 2—2.5 分的范围。但从各国及地区内教师在该指标得分上的分布看,德国、日本、墨西哥、智利仍然有部分教师没有通过课件以书面形式要求学生对特定的技能或程序进行反复训练。再看目前课程改革所重视的信息技术融入教学的设计,中国上海教师在该项课件评价指标上的表现相对偏弱,均值为 1.02,标准差仅为 0.14。尽管 GTI 项目所研究的 8 个国家及地区该项课件评分指标上的得分均偏低,但标准差最小的是中国上海。这表明上海教师在同行间很难相互学习到如何积极地把运用信息技术的机会设计到课堂教学中去。但 GTI 项目作为一项国际性的课件研究项目不仅展示了教师教学设计的多样性,还为相互学习提供了更多的可能性。在 GTI 项目课件数据库中能找到在所有课件评价指标(除"材料的准确性"外)中覆盖"低—中—高"(1—3)水平的课件样例,为国家及地区间的分享、交流与学习提供了丰富的案例来源。

(四)弥补 GTI 项目课件评价在设计上的局限性,进一步探索和提升本土化课件评价的研究水平

课件评价是 GTI 项目的组成部分,但评分人员并未使用同一套编码工具对课件和视频进行评分。尽管 11 项课件评价指标与通过视频对课进行评价的部分指标完全一致,但所评价的教师行为表现和量规却并不相同。一方面,这样的设计限制了对课件评价结果与课堂观察(如视频分析)评价结果之间进行一致性的检验,以回答课件评价对于课堂观察或视频分析是否具有增值效应。换言之,课件评价在多大程度上可以替代课堂观察或基于录像课的视频分析,或者有更优化的组合,GTI 项目课件评价无法做出回答。另一方面,这样的设计也无法基于特定的教学评价指标(如"与现实世界的联系"),对教师在课堂上实际的教学行为(视频数据)与教师在课件中设计的学习机会(课件数据)之间的相关性进行检验。而发现、衡量出设计中的课程与实施中的课程之间的鸿沟不仅有助于提升教学评价的效率,还能够更富有建设性地帮助我们找到干预教学改进的路径。这方面的研究以往都以国外研究居多,且大多是以学校或个别国家及地区为单位的本地化研究。GTI 项目课件评价在跨国及跨地区研究上做了有益的探索,但由于其设计本身的局限性,还无法从系统层面(国家及地区)对前述问题做出回应。近年来,在教育领域,视频研究已对我国课堂研究产生了重大的影响。[14]因而,在推进本土化视频研究中,我们有条件弥补GTI项目课件评价设计的局限性,为丰富课件评价的方法和理论提供地方性知识。

参考文献

[1][12][13] Martínez, J., Borko, H., & Stecher, B. Measuring Instructional Practice in Science Using Classroom Artifacts: Lessons Learned from Two Validation Studies [J]. Journal of Research in Science Teaching, 2012(1):38-67.

[2] Matsumura, L. C., Garnier, H. E., Slater, S. C., & Boston, M. D. Toward Measuring Instructional Interactions "At-scale" [J]. Educational Assessment, 2008(4):267-300.

[3][4][6][9] OECD. Global Teaching Insights: A Video Study of Teaching [R]. Paris: OECD Publishing, 2020.

[5] 徐瑾劼.以学生为主体的"参与式"课堂教学水平的跨国比较——基于OECD全球教学洞察视频研究数据的聚焦分析[J].全球教育展望,2021(1):117-128.

[7] Center for research on Evaluation, Standards, and Student Testing (CRESST). CSE Technical Report No.707 [R]. Los Angeles, CA: University of California, 2007.

[8] Brennan, R. L. Generalizability Theory [M]. New York, NY: Springer-Verlag, 2001:65.

[10] Stein, M. & Lane, S.. Instructional Tasks and the Development of Student Capacity to Think and Reason: An Analysis of the Relationship between Teaching and Learning in a Reform Mathematics Project [J]. Educational Research and Evaluation, 1996(2):50-80.

[11] Matsumura, L. C., Patthey-Chavez, G., Valdes, R., & Garnier, H. Teacher Feedback, Writing Assignment Quality, and Third-grade Students' Revision in Lower-and Higher-achieving Urban Schools [J]. The Elementary School Journal, 2002(1):3-25.

[14] 姚鹏飞,屈曼祺,李宝敏.课堂视频分析研究六十年:脉络、热点与发展趋势[J].全球教育展望,2022(3):61-77.

课堂回音与教师发展

刘良华

【摘要】传统课堂过于重视教师的讲授而较少为学生的学习提供及时的形成性评价。课堂回音是一种非正式的形成性评价。课堂回音不仅可以为学生的学习提供及时的现场反馈,还可以让学生感受到来自教师的倾听与尊重。课堂回音主要有三个策略:一是重复或归纳;二是追问或征问;三是点评或补充。课堂回音是教师专业发展的基本技能,也是评价一名教师专业发展水平的基本指标。课堂回音不仅有助于提升有效教学的质量,还是教师专业发展的有效途径。

【关键词】课堂回音;重复;追问;点评

【作者简介】刘良华/华东师范大学课程与教学研究所教授

本研究的主题是"课堂回音与教师发展",主要围绕教师如何通过"课堂回音"来推进"有效教学"和"教师发展",将重点讨论三个问题:"课堂回音与教师发展"这个课题是怎么提出来的?课堂回音有哪些理论视角?课堂回音有哪些类型?

一、课堂回音研究的由来

本研究最初关心的问题是有效教学,这是一个大课题,但可以在大课题的框架下寻找可以作为突破口的小课题。反过来说,即便关注"课堂回音"这样的小课题,大目标依然是"有效教学"。如何提高教学的效率?很多学者都做出了探索。本人的研究团队比较关注心理学家斯金纳的研究,他的女儿学习成绩不好,他申请到学校听课。听课后,斯金纳发现,教师的课堂教学有一个很大的问题:老师一个人在讲课,他无法知道学生听懂了没有。斯金纳大概会赞赏我们现在关注的"教学评一致性",但斯金纳发现,当时的教师缺乏课堂评价意识。

这正是我们关注课堂回音的原因。课堂回音为什么是重要的?因为课堂回音就是非正式的形成性评价。课堂回音关注的问题依然是如何提高教学的有效性,尤其关注如何通过非正式形成性评价的方式来提升教学的有效性。这个问题一度引起国内外教学研究者的注意。有研究者提出"提问—回应—评价"这样三段式的课堂话语结构(简称 IRE 结构),[1]也有研究者在"课堂话语"的研究中关注这个问题。[2]1993 年,奥康纳(M. O'Connor)等人发表了有关"课堂回音"的研究报告。[3]近年来,不少国内学者也开始关注课堂回音的问题。[4]有关"非正式形成性评价"的研究,也为课堂回音提供了相关的解释。[5]我们的研究聚焦于课堂回音的类型及其隐含的"非正式形成性评价"的教学价值。

中国有关"课堂回音"的研究始于2017年,这一年现在被称为中国课堂回音研究的元年。这一年,肖思汉博士出版了《听说:探索课堂互动的研究谱系》这本专著,这本书对相关领域的研究至少提供了三个方面的贡献。第一个贡献围绕课堂话语分析,课堂话语分析在2017年前后受到了普遍关注,中国教育界其实在1990年代就开始关注"课堂互动"的研究,但直到《听说:探索课堂互动的研究谱系》这本书正式出版,课堂话语分析才成为一个重要主题和关键概念。第二个贡献围绕叙事研究,中国教育界一直提倡教育叙事研究,这本书可以成为教育叙事研究的典范。就叙事研究而言,另一个值得关注的文本是《一门捉摸不定的科学:困扰不断的教育研究的历史》。[6]第三个贡献是提供了有关课堂回音的三份关键文献:一是教育学家米恩(H. Mehan)和卡兹登(C. Cazden)的研究,这一研究不仅提供了课堂回音的教育学视角,还提出了IRE模式;二是奥康纳(M. O'Connor)的研究,提供了课堂回音的语言学视角,研究者特别关注回音,在某种意义上把IRE中的E(evaluate)换成了"Rv"(revoice),IRE模式由此转换为IRRv模式;三是弗曼(E. Forman)等人的研究,最初分了四个类型,然后又增加了三个类型,共七个类型,这一分类为研究课堂回音提供了重要的帮助。

二、课堂回音对于有效教学的价值

本研究将主体教育作为课堂回音的理论视角,从主体教育的理论视角出发,课堂回音研究重点关注以下几个问题。

第一,人是客体,但也是主体。传统的教学过于重视人的客体性而忽视了人的主体性。课堂回音研究的目标之一就是激发学生的主体性,让学生发出自己的声音,让学生成为能够自学的人。

第二,人有共性,但也有差异性。以往的教学过度关注了共性,这是班级教学的优势,但班级教学容易淹没学生的个性差异。这是一个比较严重的问题,课堂回音研究的目标之二就是关注学生个别化的声音。

第三,人有理性,同时也有情绪性,或者说,人有理性,但也有情感意志。研究者较多地关注理性的知识学习,较为忽视学生的情感需要。学生在课堂里是一个需要得到尊重、需要被承认的人,课堂回音研究的目标之三就是关注学生的情感需要。

三、课堂回音的分类及其策略

研究团队参考了弗曼的分类框架,按照不交叉和不遗漏的分类原则,将课堂回音分为三个类型。这项研究为参与行动研究的学校提供了教学改革的实践策略,也为参与行动研究的大学研究者提供了实证研究的资料,有研究者在此基础上,撰写了有关课堂回音的博士学位论文。[7]研究团队将课堂回音分为三个类型。

一是重复(repeat)或归纳(summarizing)。重复虽然可能被视为比较低级的课堂回音,甚至可能被认为教师在浪费宝贵的教学时间,没有提供新的知识贡献,但是,教师重复学生的发言有多种重要的教学作用和教学价值。第一,教师在重复学生发言时,发言的学生会感受到教师在倾听学生的发言。如果没有教师投入且耐心地倾听,教师就会对学生的发言充耳不闻,对学生本人也会视而不见。没有倾听,就不会重复。教师倾听学生的发言本身就是对发言学生的尊重。第二,教师在重复学生发言时,只要教师不对所重复的某个观点表达鄙视或批评,发言的学生就会感觉自己的观点得到了老师的认可和尊重。有些教师在倾听学生发言时,会采用一边倾听一边记录的方式,记录不仅是为了接下来重复学生的观点,也是为了让发言的学生以及全班学生看到教师对学生发言的重视和尊重。第三,教师重复学生的发言,就是对这个学生的观点的认可和强化,以便全班学生重视这个学生的发言和他提出的观点。

归纳也可以视为重复的变形,与归纳相关的话语策略包括重述(restating)、转述(rephrasing)或者宣告(reporting)。重述、转述、归纳总结或宣告可视为重复的变形。如果教师选择了重述、转述或归纳总结的话语策略,那么教师就不会完整重复学生的发言,往往可能只选取学生发言的某个或某几个重要观点。归纳是对学生发言的零散观点的整理与重构,以便让发言学生以及全班其他学生获得更清晰的知识结构。

比较常见的归纳总结、重述、转述方式是重复学生发言中提到的几个关键词,通过重复关键词来重复、整理学生的观点。比如,教师面对发言的学生说:"你提到了几个关键词……"教师也可能会面向全班学生说:"张飞同学提到了几个关键词……"当教师以重复学生关键词的方式归纳总结学生的观点时,发言的学生会感受到来自老师的认可和尊重,其他学生也能从老师的归纳总结中获得更加清晰的认识。

重复的另一种方式是提升或扩展(expanding)。与提升或拓展相关的话语策略包括解读(translating)、重构(reformulation)、加工(elaboration)。比较典型的解读或加工是将学生发言中的某个观点进行抽象,将学生的具体思维提升到更高一级的高阶思维。比如,学生说:"我的旅游路线选择从广州出发,我喜欢广州。"老师在回音中对学生的观点进行加工:"哦,你是从你的经验和喜好来选择出发的地方。"学生说:"我也选择广州,因为人们就是喜欢长时间地坐火车观光。"老师在回音中对学生的观点进行加工:"哦,你是从人类行为做出的选择。"有学生说:"我统计了大家的选择,大部分人都选择了广州。"老师在回音中对学生的观点进行加工:"哦,你是根据统计得出的结论。"[8]

更有深度的提升或扩展是教师对学生发言中提到的某些观点进行提升或升华,是教师对学生提出的闪现的灵感或混乱不清的观点进行重新整理,是教师对学生发言中出现的碎片化的观点进行重构。这一做法可以让教师从学生发言的一团乱麻中理出头绪,使碎片化、一团乱麻的观点转化为有逻辑的、结构清晰的新知识。

二是追问(question)或推进(promote)。追问是对学生发言中某个观点的继续询问,让发言的学生继续发言。征询是围绕某个学生的发言,征求其他同学的意见,让其他同学继续讨论。就对话教学的对话性质而言,追问比征询更具有对话的精神。但是,在班级教学中,如果某个同学的发言已经占用了比较多的时间,征询就比追问更具有课堂对话的精神。比较典型的征询是,学生发言结束之后,教师面对全班同学提问:"张飞提出了一个重要的观点,你们听清楚他的观点了吗?你们赞成他的观点吗?"还有一种介于追问和征询之间的回音,即学生发言结束之后,教师面对这个发言的同学说:"所以,你不赞成张飞的观点?你们两个人说法好像正好相反?"这样的回音既是对发言同学的追问,也是将这个同学的观点与另外同学的观点关联起来,形成一个"共享"话题,推进学生与学生之间的对话。

三是补充或点评。补充是教师本人直接提出不同意见,虽然对话教学鼓励教师克制自己的想法,不轻易亮出自己的立场,通过延迟评判的方式来让更多学生进行头脑风暴,但是,如果正当其时,在学生普遍疑惑不解、需要倾听教师的声音的时候,教师也有责任提出自己的不同看法。点评几乎就是IRE模式中的E(评价)。对话教学需要教师延迟评判,因为教师的评判容易一锤定音而堵塞、终止其他学生的不同声音。但是,即便延迟评判,教师也还是可以抓住某个教学时机提出自己的看法,因为教师也是对话教学中的合法发言人之一。如果教师具有足够的专业智慧,即便教师与学生是平等的关系,教师也还是可以做平等中的首席。但需要注意的是,作为一种口头评价或非正式的形成性评价,教师在点评时需要谨慎,要真诚而具体地表扬学生的努力。

在所有这些课堂回音中,重复和归纳比较特殊。有研究者认为回音的重要策略是推进(advance)而不是重复。我们的理解是:重复、追问、补充其实都是"推进"。"重复"不是低级的回音,它是高级的回音。如果学生在发言时说出了十句话,教师最好能重复其中的两句或三句话,至少可以说出两个或三个关键词。如果教师能够重复学生的几句话或几个关键词,就说明教师倾听了学生的发言,对学生表示了真实的尊重。教师有时需要一边听学生发言一边做记录。做记录就是对学生发言的关注。课堂回音的前提是倾听学生,如果教师不倾听学生,教师心里只有标准答案或教案的思路,课堂回音就不可能发生。"归纳"可以视为"重复"的变形,"归纳"也是"重复"学生的关键句子或关键词。比如,一名学生说,我们班上有个同学九岁了,依然走路不稳,容易摔跤,但成绩特别好。老师说:"你是说这个孩子感统失调吗?"感统失调是一个归纳,这样的归纳是一个比较高级的推进(advance)。老师也可以说:"成绩好,走路不稳,成绩好,就是头重,走路不稳就是脚轻,合起来就是头重脚轻。"类似这样的归纳就有"推进"的价值。

课堂回音主要有以下几个价值:一是使传统的独白式教学走向对话教学;二是使传统的预设教学转向即兴教学,预设教学重视备课或教学设计,但无论教师如何备课,一旦进入真实的课堂,教师就不得不转向即兴教学;三是尊重他人,这是一种生活智慧,亲子聊天、夫妻聊天都需要回音。也因此，课堂回音不仅可以提升教学的有效性，而且可以推进教师的专业发展。

参考文献

［1］H. Mehan. Learning Lesson: Social Organization in the Classroom. Cambridge, MA: Harvard University Press, 1979.

［2］肖思汉.听说:探索课堂互动的研究谱系[M].上海:华东师范大学出版社,2017:36.

［3］M. O'Connor, S. Michaels. Aligning Academic Task and Participation Status through Revoicing: Analysis of a Classroom Discourse Strategy［J］. Anthropology & Education Quarterly, 1993(4): 318-335.

［4］郁志珍.小学科学教师回音(Revoicing)话语策略的实证研究[D].上海:华东师范大学,2019.

［5］董泽华.非正式形成性评价研究——以初中科学课堂为例[D].上海:华东师范大学,2021.

［6］[美]拉格曼.一门捉摸不定的科学:困扰不断的教育研究的历史[M].花海燕,等译.北京:教育科学出版社,2006.

［7］秦乐琦.小学数学课堂回音的话语分析[D].上海:华东师范大学,2022.

［8］肖思汉.听说:探索课堂互动的研究谱系[M].上海:华东师范大学出版社,2017:52-53.引用时对原文做了微调。

课堂分析的未来走向

国际课堂分析的十大前沿问题

石雨晨

【摘要】课堂分析领域在国内外研究界都受到了广泛关注,在过去的几十年间涌现了大量的理论和实证研究。但是,课堂分析领域的未来发展还缺乏整体的方向性指引,需要在已有研究的基础上提出前沿性问题,以推进和展望未来的研究走向。在文献研究基础上,通过展开大量的国内外专家论证和研讨,梳理了国际课堂分析的十大前沿问题。这十大问题围绕"澄清价值理论""揭示课堂真相""化数据为证据"三个方面展开,涉及了理论、分析、伦理、应用等多个角度,不仅凝练了国内外课堂分析领域的最新研究成果,还展望了课堂分析领域未来的发展趋势,有助于推动我国中小学课堂分析走在世界前列。

【关键词】课堂分析;自动化编码;伦理公约

【作者简介】石雨晨/华东师范大学课程与教学研究所副教授,所长助理

本研究旨在探索和确定课堂分析领域的十大前沿问题。为实现这一目标,研究团队经历了多个步骤的探究过程:首先,梳理了大量的已有文献,尤其是近10年的文献,并从中提炼出国内外热门课堂研究主题;其次,展开多轮内部专家论证,从先前梳理的主题中筛选出有代表性、前沿性的主题;最后,以这些问题为基础,向国外的课堂分析领域专家展开问卷调查并邀请他们提供书面意见。通过多轮迭代,研究团队最终确定了国际课堂分析领域的十大前沿问题,这些问题的发布和呈现有助于在整合已有研究的基础上,不断寻找课堂分析领域可供持续探索和创新的前沿领域,从而使得我国中小学课堂的实证研究能够走在世界前列。

整体而言,课堂分析的十大前沿问题主要围绕三个方面。第一是价值,即课堂分析需要怎样的价值引领?第二是实施和操作,课堂可能很"神秘",如何才能打开课堂黑箱,知道课堂内部到底发生了什么?第三是教学和教研,数据如何才能转化成证据,从而更好地服务于教学、教研以及其他的学校活动?下文将围绕这三个方面,呈现并分析每一个课堂分析前沿问题,旨在为今后的课堂分析和研究提供方向性的建议。

一、澄清价值理论

在澄清价值理论方面,主要提出了两大课堂分析前沿问题。第一个问题是"课堂分析需要

怎样的价值引领"。回答了这个问题也就回应了一个重要的相关问题,即什么样的课堂是好的课堂？目前看来,价值引领也好,好课的标准也好,都缺乏一个单一的、确定的答案,这一点在第20届上海国际课程论坛中也有充分的体现。本次论坛与会专家从不同的角度阐释了高质量的课堂对话应当是什么样的,有效的小组合作应当是什么样的,促进思维发展的科学论证式对话应当是什么样的,等等。所以很多时候学界并没有一个有关"好课"的统一标准。除此之外,我们还不禁要问,西方优质课堂的标准到底是否适用于我国的中小学课堂？本次论坛邀请的多名国际专家都在倡导对话、讨论、辩论、小组合作等课堂活动[1][2],但这些根植于西方教育情境的成熟经验,是否适用于我国在师生占比等教育资源上与西方课堂差异较大的课堂情境？所以这是我们需要回应的第一个问题。

如果研究者已经大致厘清了好课的标准,那么下一个问题就是"如何建构高质量的课堂分析框架"。杨晓哲副教授在本次论坛中分享了研究团队建立的高品质课堂分析标准[3],这一标准包含了三个层次,每个层次包含三个维度,因此一共是九个维度。三个层次分别是课堂效率、课堂公平和课堂民主。课堂效率包括有学、有效和有趣,有学是指学习是建构的,有效是指教学是聚焦的,有趣是指学习是愉悦的。课堂公平包含分配、程序和互动,分配是指机会是均等的,程序是指程序是正义的,互动是指对话是平等的。课堂民主包含安全、自主和合作,安全是指氛围是安全的,自主是指学习是自控的,合作是指活动是协作的。这一包含了三个层次九个维度的高品质课堂分析标准,是否真的能够帮助我们识别和区分课堂活动质量,是后续研究亟须回应的问题。

二、揭示课堂真相

在上述两个围绕价值理论问题的基础上,研究团队还从实施和操作维度提出了四个旨在逐步揭示课堂"黑箱"真相的问题。第一个问题是"如何建构多模态数据以接近课堂真相"。本次论坛中有很多报告都提到多模态数据这一理念。什么是多模态数据？多模态数据是指数据有很多类型,不仅包括言语数据,还包括非言语数据。安桂清教授和徐勤劭教授等在报告中还提到了课件、课例,这些其实也属于课堂数据[4][5]。在已有研究中,言语数据受到了更多关注。言语数据很重要,但它也只是课堂数据的一部分,课堂还包括太多其他类型的数据,包括非认知数据如情感体验、动机,行为数据如表情、动作、体态,等等。课堂通常是非常复杂的,由多个个体组成,且每个个体的内在认知和非认知活动无法直接由肉眼捕捉到。这些言语数据、文本数据、生理数据、情感数据等,又该如何获取？在神经科学领域,研究者已经开始尝试让课堂中的学生佩戴一些可穿戴设备,来捕捉他们的脑活动、心跳、皮肤电情况,以此来收集多模态数据。

如果获取多模态数据是很有必要的,另一个重要的问题就是"如何拓展多样化技术以丰富课堂数据"。杨晓哲教授在报告中提到,课堂视频的质量很重要,这将直接决定后续课堂数据的类型、数量以及质量。课堂视频质量不仅涉及音频质量,即是否能够听清楚教师和学生的语言,从而充分支持后续的转录和分析工作,还涉及画面质量,即能否从画面中清楚地看出师生的表情、神态、肢体语言等。因此,高质量的课堂数据背后离不开技术的支撑。目前国际课堂分析实验室的多所合作学校已经设置了专门的录播教室,这些教室安装了多个摄像头,能够从不同角度清晰录制教师和学生的课堂行为,甚至能够专门录制学生的小组合作行为。因此,多模态数据很重要,如何利用技术手段收集多模态数据同样非常重要。

下一个问题是:"如何提高课堂数据编码自动化水平?"本次论坛中陈高伟教授的报告以及杨晓哲教授的报告都提及了自动化编码方式。为什么自动编码非常重要?要回答这个问题,首先应明确与自动化编码相对的一个概念,即人力编码。人力编码其实对于研究者而言并不陌生,在过去的二十年间,崔允漷教授的研究团队展开了大量围绕课堂观察的研究[6],这些研究非常有价值,为课堂分析奠定了扎实的基础,但是人力毕竟是有限的,很多时候专家的数量和力量并不能很好地匹配需要分析的课堂数量。除此之外,教师和学生通常需要及时的反馈,但围绕课堂视频开展的人力分析通常要在转录、编码、统计计算等环节耗费大量的时间和精力。不难想象,如果教师无法及时获取课堂分析反馈,那么课堂分析对教与学的改进作用就是延迟的,甚至是无效的。

由此可见,自动化编码有望解放人力,极大缩短研究者转录和编码视频的时间。但是,自动化编码同样存在诸多潜在问题。例如,自动化编码可能以牺牲分析的深入,来实现分析庞大的数据。很多的已有课堂分析都是以质性研究为取向的,如肖思汉教授的报告就呈现了多个精彩的质性分析案例[7]。质性分析通常非常耗时,因此数据量可能比较小,但是它通常非常深入,能够揭示课堂及其社会文化情境中的丰富特征。与之相对应,自动化编码通常能够在短时间内处理和分析大量的数据,但是此类分析可能是低推断(low-inference),编码框架可能比较粗糙,无法精准识别细微的言语差异,而人力编码分析能够做到高推断(high-inference),从而更加深入地揭示师生的课堂活动,如学生的认知水平达到了哪个层次,学生论证时使用的证据和阐释是否充分,等等。所以自动化编码和人力编码应当是一个相辅相成的关系,它们有着各自的优势,应当结合起来使用。如果研究者需要给教师提供及时的反馈,那么自动化编码就很有必要性,但如果有必要对课堂数据开展深入分析,那么人力编码则变得不可或缺。

这一部分的最后一个问题是:"如何建设大规模、无介入的课堂分析系统?"在教室中布置录像设备也好,给教师与学生佩戴可佩戴设备也好,都是对自然状态下的教与学有侵入性的。此时,教师和学生的课堂行为与表现,无论在言语层面还是在非言语层面,都会与自然状态下的表现有差异。所以,如果我们想破解真实的课堂,如果我们想收集最"原生态"的数据,那么下一步需要思考的问题是如何无介入、常态化地收集大量的课堂数据?现有的技术水平又是否允许我们实现这一目标?如果暂不允许,那么未来我们又需要用怎样的技术手段来实现这一目标?这都是后续研究中有必要回应的重要问题。

三、化数据为证据

课堂分析的目标绝不是分析数据本身,只有当分析结果能够反馈教与学,实质提升课堂效率和质量时,课堂分析才真正发挥了其作用和价值。在化数据为证据的过程中,第一个需要回应的问题涉及伦理层面,即"课堂分析伦理公约如何建构与践行"。本次论坛的多名专家在呈现分析结果时,都把视频或图片中教师或学生的面部打码了,这其实就是在遵守课堂分析伦理公约。个体是有隐私的,儿童和未成年人作为弱势群体,保护他们的隐私尤为重要。因此,研究者如何能够在最大化捕捉、提取和分析课堂数据的同时,保护好中小学学生以及教师的人身安全及隐私?研究者应当建立怎样的课堂分析伦理公约来实现这一目标?不得不承认,我国教育学领域在伦理方面与心理学相比可能还相对滞后。心理学领域在开展研究前,都需要完成严格的伦理审核,这些审核将明确规定研究者在实验室中能够让被试做什么,以及不能让被试做什么。但是,当研究者带着录制设备进入中小学收集数据时,却很少去思考如何保护师生的隐私,如何确保后续数据不会泄露,等等。因此,课堂分析有待提升和加强在伦理方面的约束和规范,有待公布更成熟的、更有约束力的课堂分析伦理公约。

当有了强有力的伦理公约,下一个需要回应的问题是"如何用课堂数据给学生、教师画像"。画像这一概念近年来在教育研究界和实践界受到了越来越多的关注,但它仍旧存在诸多争议。有很多学者认为画像是把大量的教师和学生数据进行提取和抽象概括,在这一过程中,由于对共性的过多关注,不可避免地抹杀了个体的特质和个性。因此,在给教师和学生画像的过程中,研究者需要尽量兼顾师生的共性和特性,即如何能够在提取适用于大多数师生的信息的同时,能够最大化地保留个体差异和特殊性。

在将数据转化为证据的过程中,另一个需要回应的问题是"如何建模以满足用户教、学、评、管的需求"。对这一问题的回应正是将课堂分析结果反馈给教学的核心所在。本次论坛嘉宾陈高伟教授围绕课堂分析促进教师专业能力提升展开了深入的研究[8],他也在报告中对团队在课堂言语和对话方面的研究成果做了深入的阐释和分享。在过去的几年间,国际课堂分析实验室通过AI+OMO(artificial intelligence+online-merge-offline)项目与我国30余所中小学建立了密切的合作,目标是通过开展课堂分析并及时生成课堂分析报告,来辅助学校开展教研,并切实提升课堂教学质量。课堂分析如何促进教学、学习、评价和教研,这是中小学最关心的问题。课堂分析的数据来源于真实课堂,其分析结果也需要回归真实课堂。脱离了真实教学和教研情境,课堂分析其实就没有了生命力。因此,课堂分析以实证研究为基础,但其应用方向应当坚持实践导向,用实践效果来检验课堂分析质量。

在强调了课堂分析的实践导向以后,最后一个问题再次将理论与实践相结合,即"如何实践数据与理论的双向驱动"。课堂分析的数据虽然来自实践,但其分析导向、分析框架都要受到理论的指导。自下而上的研究属于归纳法,也就是从个体到一般,自上而下的研究属于演绎法,也就是从一般到个体。在课堂分析领域,什么是一堂好课,中西方都已经有了大量的理论研究,但实证数据又将推动研究者不断去改进和提升这些理论。国际课堂分析实验室开展的研究旨在借鉴国内和西方在课堂分析领域中的已有研究精华,通过在理论的指引下构建高质量的课堂分析标准,并开发由人工智能驱动的课堂数据分析系统,来不断回应和改进理论。以上的十个问题由研究团队经过大量的理论论证、专家研讨后得到,希望其对未来的课堂研究能够提供一定的指引,也希望今后国际课堂分析实验室能够基于更多的理论和实证研究来更好地回应这些问题。

参考文献

[1] Howe C, Abedin M. Classroom dialogue: a systematic review across four decades of research [J]. Cambridge Journal of Education, 2013,43(3):325-356.

[2] Rapanta, C., Felton, M. K. Learning to argue through dialogue: A review of instructional approaches [J]. Educational Psychology Review, 2022,34(2):477-509.

[3] 杨晓哲.基于人工智能的课堂分析架构:一种智能的课堂教学研究[J].全球教育展望,2021,50(12):55-65.

[4] 安桂清.课堂形态分析及其重构:范式转换的视角[J].教育发展研究,2023,43(4):48-55.

[5] 徐瑾劼,申昕.课件分析视域下的教与学:打开课堂教学黑箱的另一种路径——基于OECD"全球教学洞察"项目的课件评价方法及结果发现[J].全球教育展望,2022,51(10):59-71.

[6] 崔允漷.论课堂观察LICC范式:一种专业的听评课[J].教育研究,2012,33(5):79-83.

[7] 肖思汉.转轴拨弦三两声:探索中国课堂上的"回音"话语[J].全球教育展望,2022,51(10):45-58.

[8] Chen G., Clarke S. N., Resnick L. B. Classroom discourse analyzer (CDA): A discourse analytic tool for teachers [J]. Technology, Instruction, Cognition, and Learning, 2015,10(2):85-105.

基于人工智能技术的大规模课堂分析

杨晓哲

【摘要】对于课堂的观察、编码与分析由来已久。但过往的研究往往只能分析少量的课堂视频,难以实现大规模课堂分析。本研究采用人工智能技术,对1008节中小学课堂视频进行分析。分析框架采用"微观话语、中观行为、宏观课型"三个层次进行智能判定,旨在进一步揭示我国中小学课堂的教学现象。结果显示,教师讲授时间占51.9%,师生互动时间占30.5%,个人任务时间占12.3%,小组活动时间占5.3%。随着课程改革的推进,课堂一言堂现象有所减少,教师更多通过讲授与师生互动进行教学。然而,个人任务和小组活动时间仍然非常有限。此外,随着年级递增,教师提出开放性问题的频次整体呈波动递减趋势。本研究通过大规模课堂智能分析,借助大数据和自动化编码,进一步揭示了中小学课堂的教学现象。

【关键词】课堂分析;人工智能;教学现象

【作者简介】杨晓哲/华东师范大学课程与教学研究所副教授

一、问题的提出

"课堂"是根据一定的目标,在教师的设计与引导下,展开教与学过程的主要时空。课堂提供了一个理解与研究教育活动和学习本质的重要场域,为教育研究者挖掘教学现象提供了重要的切入口。对课堂教学进行有效的分析与评价,不仅可以帮助教师了解课堂中的学生学习,也可以关注真实的教育教学实践,并能够同时促进教师自我与群体的专业发展。课堂经由师生多主体的共同创生而成,却往往难以被完全理解。不仅是课堂局外人难以看懂课堂,而且身处课堂中的教师与学生也很难完全理解课堂本身。长期以来,课堂的真实状况被形象地称之为"黑箱"。绝大多数的研究仅针对有限的几节课或几十节课展开分析,缺乏关于大规模课堂的实证研究。基于大数据的具有普遍意义的中国课堂是什么样的,到底存在哪些教学现象?课程改革发展至今,中国中小学课堂目前的现状与面貌如何?这些问题无法仅从有限的印象或经验进行回答,也很难通过思辨给出客观回应。

因此,通过对课堂视频的大量分析研究,采用技术方式实现定量统计与综合分析。从课堂的个案分析到大规模课堂的规律探寻,是当前我国课程改革的迫切所需。在回答"中国的课堂是什么样的"的问题时,对课堂视频的深度描绘往往受到人力成本高、依赖专家学者、人工编码效率低、难以规模化等因素限制。如何借助智能技术,尤其是基于人工智能技术实现数据化、证据化的课堂分析尤为重要。本研究采用人工智能技术,对大规模课堂进行自动编码分析,根据课堂分析统计结果,进一步归纳我国大规模课堂中的教学言语、教学行为、课堂类型等特征,从而探究基于证据的大规模课堂教学现象。

二、研究设计

(一) 研究思路

本研究采用团队开发的"高品质课堂智能分析系统"。该系统架构包含数据层、认知层、标准层、应用层[1]。数据层包含言语数据等在内的多模态数据,系统微观层面的判定依据来源于此;中观与宏观层面的判定则基于认知层的构建。具体而言,就是通过数据库所采集的大量语料与图像,进行机器学习,构建一个课堂对话与行为的自动分类模型,将处理好的数据分类用于模型训练并得到最优模型。最后使用模型实现课堂话语与行为的分类识别与判定。本研究采用"高品质课堂智能分析系统"对1008节中小学语文课堂视频数据进行分析,对课堂教学现象进行分层解构。

(二) 分析与编码框架

本研究从微观层面、中观层面和宏观层面对课堂的教学现象进行分析、描绘和统计。三类编码与判定的依据如图1所示:

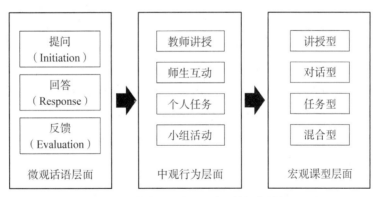

图1 课堂微观—中观—宏观的智能判定

1. 微观话语层面

对课堂中的师生对话进行编码分析。采用课堂对话编码的经典结构IRE,即教师提问(Initiation)、学生回答(Response)和教师反馈(Evaluation)[2]。为了更加深入地描绘课堂对话及其质量,研究者在IRE结构的基础上进一步构建出了IRE分水平模型,关注课堂对话中封闭式、推理性、开放式的不同层级提问、回答和反馈。以"提问"的水平划分及其编码为例,"有标准答案的封闭式简短问题"判定为水平一,编码为I1;"有标准答案的推理性或解释性问题"判定为水平二,编码为I2;"无标准答案的开放式或半开放式问题"判定为水平三,编码为I3。进而,通过基于IRE的三类水平(水平一、水平二、水平三)进行深度学习算法训练,实现人工智能能够对IRE进行判定,并分别区分IRE三类的三个不同水平,从而实现课堂师生对话的自动分水平话语编码。

2. 中观行为层面

对课堂行为划分为不同的时段类型。基于课堂中教师和学生的行为表现,有学者将课堂教学形态分为了三种类型:一是教师告诉学生型,即教师向学生传授知识和技能;二是教师和学生对话型,即教师和学生之间开展师生互动;三是教师指导学生学习型,即学生在教师的指导下开展自主与合作学习。在此基础上,本研究进一步将第三种课堂教学形态细分为学生个人任务和学生小组活动,由此划分出一堂课的四种行为时段类型,分别是教师讲授、师生互动、个人任务、小组活动。采取人工智能分析技术,能够实现对课堂中的师生行为进行分类型多角度识别,诸如课堂中的学生听讲、学生小组讨论、教师讲解板书等行为。再综合采取声纹识别技术,能够实现区分课堂中的教师与学生的话语,结合多模态数据判定的结果从而确定课堂中的四种时段类型。

3. 宏观课型层面

对课堂进行定性判断,判定课堂类型。S—T(Student—Teacher)分析法是计算课堂类型的经典方案,在这种分析方法中,课堂教学行为被分为了学生(S)行为和教师(T)行为,然后根据T行为占有率(Rt)以及T行为与S行为的转换率(Ch)判断课堂所属类别[3]。Rt和Ch的取值范围都为0到1,Rt数值越大代表教师行为占比越多,Ch数值越大代表师生互动越多。根据Rt和Ch的值,S—T分析法将课堂类型分为了讲授型($Rt>0.7$)、对话型($Ch>=0.4$)、任务型($Rt<=0.3$)、混合型($0.3<Rt<0.7$同时满足$Ch<0.4$)。讲授型是以教师讲授为主的课堂;对话型是以师生之间进行话语交流为主的课堂;任务型是课堂中以自主学习任务、协作小组任务为主的课堂;混合型则是较为综合类型的一种课堂形态。

(三) 数据来源与分析处理

本研究的课堂视频数据来自项目组采集的全国公开课的课堂视频数据。本研究选取其中的语文学科视频为研究对象,包括1至9年级,共计9个年级的语文课堂教学视频数据。每个年级共计112节语文课,共计1008节,视频总时长约674小时。本研究采用了视频分析法、内容分析法、统计分析法等研究方法。利用人工智能技术实现了课堂师生对话语义内容的自动分类与自动编码,对数据的分析主要包含:描述性量化分析(包括频次、均值、百分比等数值)、单因素方差分析(判断不同均值间是否存在显著性差异)等统计方法。

三、课堂教学现象的发现

本研究通过使用"高品质课堂智能分析系统",对1 008节课堂教学视频进行微观话语、中观行为、宏观课型分析,基于数据与证据,发现以下课堂教学现象。

(一)微观话语现象:课堂师生对话

经过系统智能分析后的统计数据表明,在1 008节语文课中,教师每节课的平均提问个数(I)为81.43个,学生每节课平均回答个数(R)为55.74个,教师对学生的反馈回应(E)的个数为43.81个。换而言之,教师平均每节课提出约80个问题。以40分钟为一节课估算,则平均1分钟提问个数为2个。研究发现,其中许多问题并不需要学生在课堂上进行回答。在某种程度上,教师提出的多数问题属于自问自答类型或只是要求学生进行简单的点头回应。中小学课堂中教师普遍出现频繁发问的课堂教学现象。

针对教师提问进行分水平编码分析得出,教师多数问题集中在水平一和水平二。教师每节课平均提出水平一的问题是32.11个,水平二的问题是44.32个,水平三的问题是5个。由此可见,教师多数提出简单问题或有标准答案的问题,而对无标准答案的开放式或半开放问题较少提出。教师对于学生的反馈理答也多集中在水平一和水平二,均值分别为20.43个和20.71个,水平三的回应每节课平均仅有2.67个。因此,在师生对话分水平分析中,我国课堂呈现一种"教师更多封闭式提问与简洁回应"的现象。教师具有较好的提问意识,但开放性问题较少,教师也会时常反馈回应学生的回答,但是进一步促进学生反思或元认知的反馈相对较少。

进一步对分年级的师生互动话语数据进行统计分析(如图2所示),并对9个年级中的师生互动话语数量进行方差分析发现:在教师提问方面,八年级、九年级的提问数量较多,每节课平均提问数量分别为100.7个和109.8个,其中九年级的提问数量显著高于其他年级($p<0.001$),八年级的提问数量显著高于一至七年级($p<0.001$)。

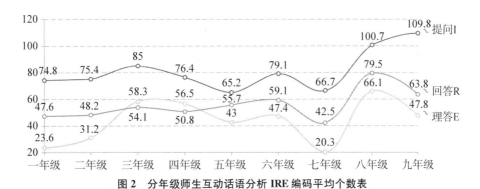

图2 分年级师生互动话语分析IRE编码平均个数表

再对水平三的提问进行分年级统计,呈现出平均个数从一年级到九年级波动递减的趋势(如图3所示)。其中,九年级水平三的提问平均个数显著低于一、二、四、六年级($p<0.01$)。随着年级的递增,开放性提问的个数呈现显著的波动递减趋势。可见,初中教师更倾向于选择封闭、安全的课堂提问内容与方式,而非采用更开放、更具有挑战性的问题来激发学生参与对话与互动。这也揭示了一种矛盾的现象。一般而言,更高年级的学生具有相对更高的认知复杂度,即初中生相较于小学生的认知能力更高。但研究却发现真实的课堂中,面对更高认知复杂度的初中生,教师反而选择了更封闭、更简单、更安全的问题居多。该矛盾表明,课堂提问的开放度并没有符合学生的认知发展规律。

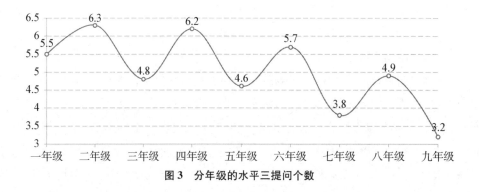

图3　分年级的水平三提问个数

(二) 中观行为现象:课堂时间分布

通过对课堂中的行为进行综合分析,可以判定一节课中哪些时间段属于哪种类型。经分析统计数据显示,1 008节课中"教师讲授"时间平均占比达到51.9%,"师生互动"的时间平均占比30.5%,"个人任务"占比12.3%,"小组活动"占比5.3%。假若取该平均占比数据,构建一节标志性中国中小学课堂,以40分钟为一节课计算,那么这节课的课堂时间分布近似为教师讲授21分钟、师生互动12分钟、个人任务5分钟、小组活动2分钟。

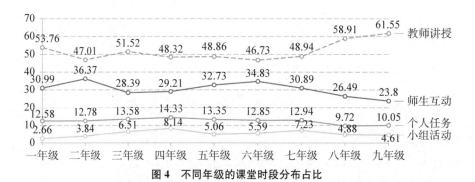

图4　不同年级的课堂时段分布占比

从一年级到九年级的视角来看,平均每节课的课堂时段分布占比如图4所示。二年级的

"教师讲授"时长占比最低(占比为47.01%),九年级占比最高(占比为61.55%)。在对9个年级中的课堂活动时段进行方差分析后发现:一年级、八年级与九年级的"教师讲授"时长显著高于其他年级($p<0.001$)。一年级、二年级、八年级与九年级的"个人任务"占比时长显著低于三年级、四年级($p<0.001$)。"小组活动"中一年级占比时长最低,为2.66%,显著低于三年级、四年级、六年级与七年级($p<0.001$)。

课堂时间分布与占比不仅意味着不同的教学组织方式,也直接影响着学生们的学习方式。本研究从数据上验证了人们心中"小学课堂更多互动,中学课堂更多讲授"的直观经验。研究发现,七年级、八年级、九年级的初中语文教师在讲授时间占比上逐级增加。并且,师生互动、个人任务和小组活动的占比不断减少。

(三) 宏观课型现象:课堂类型现状

依据上述分类,经过对1008节课的人工智能分析,可判断每节课的课堂类型,并将课堂划分为四种类型。综合来看,不同年级均出现了四种不同的课堂类型,其中混合型课堂在各年级中最为普遍,占比71.8%,任务型课堂占比12%,对话型课堂占比8.3%,讲授型课堂占比7.8%。对九个年级的课堂类型进行统计分析和可视化呈现(如图5所示),图中每个点代表一节课,并置于坐标中表明该课的课堂类型。

结果表明,年级越高,讲授型课堂的占比越高。然而,随着学生认知发展,原本应随年级增

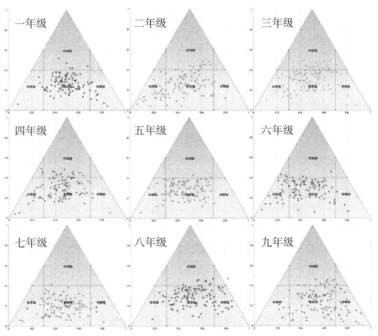

图5 不同年级的课堂类型分布

加的深度互动课堂类型却减少了。从各年级的课堂类型来看,整体而言,课堂类型与年级之间并没有显著的相关性,课堂类型的整体分布保持较为稳定的占比。

四、结论与讨论

本研究利用人工智能技术揭示课堂教学现象,洞悉课堂教学存在的规律,是一次打开课堂"黑箱"的尝试。从方法上为课堂编码与分析提供了进一步自动化、规模化的技术路径,从结果上为描述我国中小学课堂教学现象提供了客观数据与证据。

(一)我国中小学语文课堂教学的群像

本研究运用人工智能技术分析了1008节中小学语文课堂视频,为了解中国课堂教学现象提供了大规模数据与证据,描绘了课堂教学现象的一般群像。

在课堂时段的分布上,随着我国课程改革的深化发展,我国中小学语文课堂中出现满堂灌的现象明显减少。从均值占比而言,课堂中教师讲授时间占比51.9%。整体来看,教师已经关注到了课堂是一个学习展开的历程,是一个师生互动的过程。教师并没有完全陷入一言堂的模式中,并把时间留给了师生互动。课堂中的师生互动对话的时间占比为30.5%。从微观的课堂言语分析可以进一步得出,虽然教师在课堂中提出了大量的问题,但是问题的类型通常缺乏变化,多以知识记忆再现、刺激内容回顾、班级教学管理为主要目标。教师在课堂中以提出低阶问题为主,这和以往研究的结论相同,即教师在课堂中普遍采用"数量多、简单化"的提问方式[4]。这些特点表明,当前中小学语文课堂教学已关注并展开了师生对话的过程,但是一问一答的简单模式居多,课堂对话的深度与开放度有待进一步提升。从课堂中"个人任务"时间占比12.3%和"小组活动"时间占比5.3%可以看出,课堂中可以让学生展开差异化、自主化、协作化的学习时间仍然极其有限和局促。特别是小组合作时间,平均一节课不足2分钟,学生的合作精神和合作能力很难常态化持续提升。再就不同年级的课堂而言,尽管高年级的课堂出现了更多讲授,更少开放性问题的现象,但是总体来看,随着年级的递增,课堂整体类型趋于稳定,课堂样态基本不变。

(二)更大规模的尺度更精细的编码

如何通过更大规模的课堂分析,更精细有效地课堂编码分析与理解课堂,始终是教育教学研究的难题。以往依靠人力和专家对课堂进行分析的方式,几乎无法完成大量的课堂编码与分析工作。而本研究采用的"微观话语—中观行为—宏观课型"的三层智能判定,使得研究者可以对上千节课进行分析与统计研究,以揭秘学生学习规律,洞悉中国课堂的教学现象。从经验中的直观印象到基于更大规模的客观数据,这是本研究借助人工智能技术的重要突破所在。

与此同时,本研究仍存在一些局限,首先是如何平衡课堂视频录制中的"常态化"与"精品化"之间的关系。本研究扩大了数据数量与来源范围,尽可能多地收集更多的课堂视频。但是,我们仍需关注的是,当教师和学生进入一个摄像录像的教室中,难免会受到情绪、认知、干预等影响,造成一定的偏差。其次,由于课堂是一个复杂且动态的过程与场域,研究和理解教师与学生之间的对话以及学习活动是一个相当宽广的实践挑战。我们仍要保有人的专业判断介入,而非机械地将课堂拆分到固定的框架中,警惕部分算法和偏差性数据带来的误判,避免陷入技术主义。

尽管本研究相较于其他课堂分析的研究,已经在课堂课节数据量上有了显著的提升,但是上千节课的课堂数据统计与分析结果所发现和推倒的教学现象仍需要不断求证。研究者仍需反思什么样的数据规模才能够真正揭示课堂教学现象中的本质规律。通过人工智能技术,研究者能够人机协同地实现更大规模的课堂多模态分析,能够实现更精细化的课堂自动化编码,为进一步揭示课堂背后的规律性现象提供了新的路径。

参考文献

[1] 杨晓哲.基于人工智能的课堂分析架构:一种智能的课堂教学研究[J].全球教育展望,2021,50(12):55-65.

[2] MEHAN H. "What time is it, Denise?": asking known information questions in classroom discourse [J]. Theory into practice, 1979,18(4):285-294.

[3] 傅德荣,章慧敏.教育信息处理[M].北京:北京师范大学出版社,2001:94-108.

[4] 王陆,彭功.2015—2019年中小学课堂高阶问题特征图谱[J].电化教育研究,2020,41(10):65-72.

How Can We Equip Teenagers with Skills and Values of Reasoned and Respectful Discourse?

Professor Deanna Kuhn

Teachers College, Columbia University

Abstract

Our world is facing new and frightening challenges, and political polarization has never been greater. Many see reasoned, respectful discourse as our only path to survival and progress, but attaining the skills and values it requires is not straightforward. Professor Deanna Kuhn of Columbia University has developed a discourse-based curriculum to help the next generation develop the values and the social and critical thinking skills they will need if they are to use tools of discourse to address the complex problems and challenges that await them.

Keywords: argumentation; dialogue; discourse; teenager

In today's troubled world, many of us see reasoned discourse between participants of goodwill as our only hope. Belief in reasoned discourse is a pillar of democracy, but will it be capable of saving us? There is much working against it. The media provides us with talking heads who represent the extremes at either end of the political continuum. What they spout is less discourse than it is strident, ever louder diatribes that don't address their opponent's position except to dismiss it. The result is a turn-off to most listeners. They accept their favored speaker's claims uncritically, while the opponent's screed is too irritating and their alleged facts and figures too wearying to contemplate.

Nor do these media rants change anyone's views. If anything, listeners feel a greater press to define themselves. They do so simply by identifying the tribe they belong to. This identity is sufficient to explain their position to others and even themselves: "I hold this view because of who I am and connect to." Tribe members are not inclined to seek to enrich or sharpen their views through reflecting, alone or with others.

Professor Deanna Kuhn of Columbia University has developed a discourse-centered approach to improve things. Researchers are now investing significant time and resources to understand what will change people's views. Kuhn's approach has a different goal: helping individuals to enrich their views by enriching the thinking that underlies them. If people aren't inclined to seek such enrichment for themselves, this is not a straightforward task. Introducing new ideas by getting people to engage personally with those with different opinions and values is difficult to achieve. If emotions and group identity are already running high, even careful listening may be out of reach, much less productive discourse, and doing so comes with the risks of further extremism and greater entrenchment in one's own position.

Discussion with like-minded people carries its own, similar risks, but it can lead to some modest enrichment of thinking. Simply being asked to explain one's view can be beneficial, yet too much explaining can reinforce commitment to a position. It carries the further risk of simplification rather than enrichment. For example, Kuhn asked people about letting undocumented immigrants who entered the US unknowingly as children to stay in the country. Of those who favored letting them stay, she further probed whether this approval should extend to near and then even distant relatives. Rather than attempt the difficult distinctions required, some responded, "Just let them all stay."

This finding led Kuhn's research team to a potentially productive middle ground between probing one's own ideas and engaging in dialog with someone who holds contrasting views. This middle ground proved successful, even when individuals are no more than passive listeners rather than themselves engaged in dialog. Furthermore, observing a rich, well-reasoned dialog between speakers holding opposing positions proved more powerful in enriching a listener's thinking than listening to the same speakers presenting individual positions containing the same ideas. This difference, pointing to the power of dialog, appeared among both college students and community adults.

As one part of the discourse curriculum for young teens that Kuhn and her team have developed, participants individually create their own written dialogs between two speakers holding opposing views on a topic being studied. The format forces students to continually shift perspectives, from one to the other hypothetical speaker. These constructed dialogs have proven richer in ideas and in reasoning compared to conventional written essays, pointing to their value as a learning tool.

While individually constructed dialogs are productive, they are no replacement for individuals engaging first-hand in discourse with one another on significant issues. Discourse-based activities are currently viewed favorably among many teachers, but too often they take the form of teacher-centered whole-class discussions that consist simply of a teacher eliciting a succession of students' opinions. Kuhn's curriculum has participants engage directly, one-on-

one or at most two-on-two, with a succession of different partners who hold contrasting, or sometimes similar, positions. This decenters the teacher as the channel through which discourse flows, and it enables students to practice the discourse skills that develop.

Participants engage in debate about significant issues, beginning with the personal and then extending to their communities, nation, and world: Should a teenager get work experience during high school years? Is space exploration or aid to poor nations good uses of a society's resources? Students engage deeply with a topic, over successive occasions. Topics are ones that even a few initially skeptical participants quickly come to care about, and all choose their own positions. Typically, dialogs take place electronically, providing a record that promotes review and reflection. Dialogs quickly come to show energy and purpose. Participants very soon recognize that they need to address one another's claims, drawing on evidence and arguments to support and to challenge them. During these dialogs, students are "on duty" 100 ％ of the time. They cannot relax into the passive listener role frequently seen in whole-classroom discussions. The teacher meanwhile relinquishes a role of authority as the source of knowledge and replaces it with shared construction of meaning and another basis for authority-that of evidence and argument.

Through sustained engagement and practice, students gain an increased sense of responsibility to one another. They come to embrace the norms of discourse, beginning with the close attention and relevant responses that a dialog partner comes to expect. Claims are expected to have reasons, and these must stand to the challenge of strong argument and potentially weakening evidence. In time, students come to feel the empowerment of entering a community of discourse. They come to recognize and value the purpose and power of authentic discourse as worth the investment and energy it entails.

Kuhn and her team focus their efforts on young people, as those who hold the future of civilization and democracy in their hands. Most recently, today's technology has made it feasible for the team to extend their approach across international borders. They have organized a series of electronic dialogs between an American teen and a counterpart in mainland China. Although initially hesitant to become involved, schools in China made the opportunity available to families, who quickly became enthusiastic, as did the young participants in both countries.

Participants' reflections after just a week of daily dialog with two new partners each day were overwhelmingly positive. One American teen said, "The fact that I was able to communicate with and have real-time conversations with people halfway across the world really stood out to me and is an experience I'll never forget." "American teens are friendly," a

Chinese teen remarked. Another one noted, "Talking to new people each day allowed me to hear new ideas and perspectives." And an American teen even expressed his awareness that "the evidence and the claims they were making started to make me question my opinion." All wanted the dialogs to continue.

This experiment offers us a key lesson: Transforming the unknown into the known and familiar may not be difficult, and doing so can have potentially far-reaching consequences. Those who shape the future of U.S.-China relations, and indeed influence international relations worldwide, will be of a new generation of young people around the globe. They are now constructing their own images of the major players on the world stage and how they relate to one another.

Getting people on opposite sides of the backyard fence, and even the world, into productive conversations with one another, allowing them to discover who those others are, stands to reduce the sense of menace and potential threat that "otherness" confers. Kuhn and her team's curriculum offers a path for teens to develop the values and the skills of discourse. Preparing them to do so may be our best hope to save a precarious world.

Related publications

Kuhn, D., Bruun, S., & Geithner, C. (2024), Enriching thinking through discourse. *Cognitive Science, 48.* https://doi.org/10.1111/cogs.13420.

Kuhn, D., & Modrek, A. (2021). Mere exposure to dialogic framing enriches argumentive thinking. *Applied Cognitive Psychology, 35,* 1349-1355.

Kuhn, D. (2023). The future of U.S.-Chinese relations lies with a new generation. *Journal of International Social Studies Education, 13,* 70-73.

Kuhn, D. (2018). *Building our best future: Thinking critically about ourselves and our world.* New York: Wessex Learning. *(written for a teen audience)*

Kuhn, D., Feliciano, N., & Kostikina, D. (2019). Engaging contemporary issues as practice for citizenship. *The Social Studies, 110,* 1-13.

Kuhn, D. (1991). *The skills of argument.* New York: Cambridge University Press.

Shi, Y., Matos, F., & Kuhn, D. (2019). Dialog as a bridge to argumentative writing. *Journal of Writing Research. 11,* 107-129. DOI:10.17239/jowr2019.11.01.04.

Zavala, J., & Kuhn, D. (2017). Solitary discourse is a productive activity. *Psychological Science, 28,* 578-586.

Elnakouri, A., Huynh, A. C., & Grossmann, I. (2024). Explaining contentious political issues promotes open-minded thinking. *Cognition, 247, 105769.*

Lee, C. D., White, G., & Dong, D. (Eds.). (2021). *Educating for civic reasoning and discourse.* Washington, DC: National Academy of Education.